MW01493778

Writing Your Story for God's Glory

A Memoir Workbook

C. S. Lakin

Writing Your Story for God's Glory: A Memoir Workbook

Copyright©2017 by C. S. Lakin

Cover designed by C. S. Lakin and Ellie Searl, Publishista®

All rights reserved.

No part of this publication may be reproduced, distributed, or transmitted in any form or by any means, including photocopying, recording, or other electronic or mechanical methods, without the prior written permission of the publisher, except in the case of brief quotations embodied in critical reviews and certain other noncommercial uses permitted by copyright law.

ISBN-978-0-98613-475-3

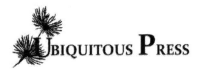

Ubiquitous Press
Morgan Hill, CA

Writing Craft Books by C. S. Lakin

Table of Contents

Introduction

Stories are powerful. Humans since the dawn of creation have been telling stories—their stories. Stories of family and ancestry. Stories of valor and fear. Stories of victory and defeat. We are a species of storytellers. God made us in his image to be creative beings, and storytelling is an expression of creativity.

Any story, whether fictional or true, has the power to evoke emotion, move people to action, change hearts and lives. Words via stories are the way we express our abstract thoughts, our dreams, and our hopes, as well as comfort others.

Words are so powerful that God Himself used them as His means of creation. He spoke, and through those words brought worlds into existence. He chose to make Himself known to humans in two specific ways: through His visible creation and through a collection of stories that humans, inspired by the Holy Spirit, penned so that we might know this unfathomable and indefinable Creator of the universe.

That's how important and powerful words are.

If God is moving in your heart to tell your story—whether for yourself, your family, or others—it's time to bring your words into existence.

It's time to write your memoir.

Writing a book can be a daunting endeavor. A book is a big project, but, as with all big projects, it can be approachable and manageable if it's broken down into smaller pieces. As the saying goes: How do you eat an elephant? One bite at a time.

And one thing that may help you push past your trepidation to write is to think of yourself as a storyteller instead of an author. In the tradition of all our ancestors, you and I—everyone on Earth—are storytellers.

This isn't anything new or difficult. You tell stories all the time. You rush to your girlfriends to tell them about the crazy guy who almost crashed into your car. You gush about how your son made the winning touchdown in his playoff game. You tell your husband over dinner how your day went, detailing how you managed to get your boss to give you a raise.

If typing words or writing with a pen on paper freezes you up, consider recording yourself recounting the stories of your life. Pretending you are talking to your closest friend. Use whatever method helps free up your mind and heart to enable you to delve into your past.

As you "replay" in your mind the specific incidents from that time that you want to share in your memoir, close your eyes, start at the beginning, and describe the scene, your feelings, who and what was around you, the smell of the air and the feel of the weather. If you immerse yourself into that moment and bring it to life, you will immerse your readers as well.

Memoir vs. Autobiography

Memoirs are a slice of life. A story from your life. They aren't the entire account of your life but center on a specific time in which something significant happened. If you want to write the story of your life, that's an autobiography, and while much of what is presented in this workbook can be applied to writing an autobiography, know that they are two different things.

You can write many memoirs. Think of the journey of a woman who studies hard to be the first in her family to graduate college. Or be the first woman of color to serve as a judge in her county. Or consider the person who ventures out for a month to help starving children in a war-torn country or aid in a hurricane rescue of people or animals. Each of these could be the subject and content of a full memoir.

No doubt you could think of a capsule of time in which you began a journey, whether spiritual, emotional, or actual (or all three). Any experience that you've had in which you grew, learned, changed, and possibly impacted others in a significant way holds potential for memoir.

Because of this, you don't have to have lived a long full life in order to tell the story that is on your heart. You could be a high school student who spent a year abroad in an exchange program. You could be a college student who stood up and spoke out when injustices broke out on campus.

And, in contrast, some women have penned their memoirs well into their eighties, and even later. Age is not a consideration when it comes to telling a powerful, important, or even just amusing story.

When we write a memoir, we go on a journey of discovery—of awareness, acceptance, understanding, and sometimes healing. Memoir is a search for self, but your memoir is not the attempt to answer "Who am I?" but "Who am I *in this story*?"

Writing Honestly

Writing an honest memoir takes some thought (we'll be going into your storyteller's voice and attitude further on) and time. We need to practice, develop, and refine our writing skills so that the memories we draw from our hearts and minds and place on the page accomplish what we intend. We don't want our word to go out "void," without impacting our readers.

Through memoir we share things that normally don't come out in everyday conversation. We sometimes share things we often don't think about. And we may even share things we very much don't want to think about.

The journey into memoir is a journey deep into the heart. It's a journey into the past, and sometimes that's a past we would rather forget, one that holds pain.

Writing memoir requires us to both delve into those memories as well as insulate ourselves from them. Writing honestly means summoning courage to speak truth, yet it allows for some embellishment or censorship as needed. Only you can decide what "writing honestly" encompasses.

Be patient, be prayerful, be reflective, be humble, be teachable, be open to what this process may reveal to you. As you work to honestly communicate your story, God will work in your heart. The Spirit that dwells in us guides our hand and heart in all our creative endeavors.

As with everything, we are to "be anxious for nothing, but in everything, by prayer and supplication with gratitude, make [our] requests known to God" (Phil. 4:6 Modern English Version).

That is how we are able to write our story for God's glory.

How to Use This Book

This memoir workbook is not intended to be an instructional manual for writing composition. While you will learn many helpful writing techniques to aid you in telling a powerful and coherent story, you won't learn the all the nuts and bolts of composition.

Consider taking classes at a nearby college or learning center, as well as getting books on writing, if you need to work on your writing skills. It's important to know how to write sentences well and use grammar and punctuation correctly.

But don't let a lack of expertise hold you back from writing your story. Do your best, perhaps get editing help from a professional or friend with strong writing skills. Don't self-sabotage your calling to write your story because of your fear or insecurities. God can and will make up for your lack, and it's in our weakness that He is strong. Meaning, put the work in, pray, trust God, ask for His help and direction, and push aside the stumbling blocks and excuses.

If you struggle with distractions and excuses and self-doubt, consider reading *Crank It Out! The Surefire Way to Become a Super-Productive Writer.* While you might not have interest in cranking out lots of memoirs, the methods and insights in that book will show you how to hack through the barriers preventing you from writing, both internal and external.

Write in this workbook! That's what it's for. However, space is limited (for obvious reasons), so if you find the need to write more than space allows, have at hand a blank journal, a notepad, or an open Word document on your computer. Don't let the limited space in this workbook keep you from jotting down what comes into your head.

You don't need to work through the workbook in order, although you might find it to be the most logical way to learn the material. Feel free to skip around and work on sections that interest you in the moment.

There is so much more to writing memoir than can be included in this workbook. Consider buying or borrowing (from your local library or via an online ebook lending service) memoirs and studying them (you'll find a list at the end of this book). You can learn so much from analyzing the components of great books: writing style, structure, tone, dialogue, and much more.

Are you ready to begin? Then turn the page and get started on your new writing journey!

Part 1: Before You Begin

Chapter 1: Questions to Ponder before You Begin

As with any book, it's helpful to put together an outline of what you plan to write about. But before you can get to that point in the writing process, you need to understand how to tell a powerful, moving story and what thwarts that attempt.

And most importantly, you need to ask questions.

Creating a structure for your memoir is not about reinventing the wheel. You can and should base your structure off of memoirs that have already been written, though you may feel the best structure for your memoir is a unique one. Regardless, before you dig into telling your story, do your homework. Read memoirs that sound as if they might be similar to yours.

Think about the tone of your story. Will it be humorous? Snarky? Dead serious? Intense? A mixture of all these?

Is your story about overcoming? Surviving a tragedy or horrible situation? The tone you set for your story matters greatly. If you've found that humor was what helped you get through, then you'll want to bring that humor into your story without making light of your suffering or others'.

If yours is an uproarious account of some period in your life, by all means, make it funny. But consider including the heavy, serious moments that bridge those times.

Some memoirs are wild rides that take the reader through hilarious moments to horribly tragic ones. They are a journey of experience, often a unique or amazing one, and the purpose of the telling is to entertain, enlighten, inspire and/or instruct.

It's important for you to decide, before you begin, *on your purpose.*

Maybe you want to write your story as a cathartic experience, and you don't intend to share it with anyone (or more than a few people). That's perfectly fine, and it can be extremely healing.

Maybe you want to write your story to help others who might be going through what you went through. In that case, you have a specific audience you are writing to.

Anytime you aim to sell a book to consumers (readers), you need to define and target your niche audience. And that requires some homework to figure out who that audience is and the best way to write your book to appeal to them.

And where will you begin your tale? Start thinking about *why* you want to write your memoir, for *whom*, and *what* take-home message or feeling (theme) you want to leave readers with.

What do I mean by a "take-home" message? It's the emotion, reflection, or truth you want readers to feel they've learned and experienced through your story. It's the thought that lingers in their mind long after they finish reading your memoir. You may have many such moments in your memoir, but when readers close the book, they will have an overall feeling about the story they just read.

All this, of course, may change once you get into writing. But it's a place to start.

What kind of story is yours?

Spend a few minutes thinking about these questions, then write down your thoughts.

Who is my audience? What type of reader will be interested in and benefit by my story? Why?

_____

_____

_____

_____

_____

What is the reason I want to write my memoir?

_____

_____

_____

_____

_____

_____

_____

_____

_____

What kind of tone do I want to set?

_____

_____

_____

_____

_____

_____

_____

What emotions do I hope to evoke in readers as they read my story?

_____

_____

_____

_____

_____

_____

_____

What is the take-home message or conclusion I want to leave with my readers?

_____

_____

_____

_____

_____

_____

_____

_____

_____

_____

_____

_____

_____

_____

Writing Prompt:

"After everything I went through, the most important lesson I learned was. . ."

_____

_____

_____

_____

_____

_____

_____

_____

_____

_____

_____

_____

_____

_____

Chapter 2: Your Unique Story

You may feel as if your story isn't anything special. You aren't famous or influential. Your story, to you, sounds like a thousand other stories.

But here's the thing: no one has had your exact life or experienced exactly what you experienced.

But many, many people have gone through or are going through something *similar* to what you have. As humans, we share, universally, the human experience.

Think What You Have in Common with Others

Everyone—whether old or young, black or white, rich or poor, or living in the US or Antarctica—needs shelter, food, love, understanding, employment, security, and good health. When you focus your theme on a basic need, readers will relate. These are universal issues, universal themes.

God has put your story into your heart for you to tell, and your story matters. Readers are drawn in to truthful stories from the heart, and if you share your story honestly, humbly, with passion, conviction, and a desire to inspire, your story will be just as valid, meaningful, even important as anyone else's.

So keep in mind: your story isn't about you. It's about something bigger. Think long and hard about what that "bigger thing" is. Ask God to help you find and voice your story so others will be uplifted.

For example, if your theme underlying your memoir is telling readers: "You aren't alone. I've gone through this very thing, and I've come out victorious. If I can do it, you can too," then you will have a powerful story.

We'll get further into theme, but first consider this:

How is my story unique? List aspects of your story that make it different from any other story "out there."

_____

_____

_____

_____

_____

_____

_____

_____

_____

_____

How is my story like many other stories, and why will it resonate with many people? Who will it resonate with?

_____

_____

_____

_____

_____

_____

_____

_____

_____

_____

_____

Understanding Your Motivation

Your motivation for telling your story is crucial to understand. Why? Because if you are writing for *the wrong reasons*, you will only sabotage your story.

What are some wrong reasons?

- *Payback or vengeance.* When we've been hurt or abused or treated unfairly, it's only natural to feel a desire to vent and even retaliate through exposure.

- *To wallow in the pain.* Wallowing is akin to whining. And neither of those leads to healing ourselves or building up others.

The place to vent, rage, whine, or wallow is in prayer to God, who welcomes our pain and stores all our tears in a bottle. Journaling is another way to privately express these tumultuous feelings without bringing them into existence in the world of other humans.

There is a difference between wallowing and bearing witness. Think of yourself in the role of storyteller *as the mature self* that bears witness to the events of your life instead of as the victim who has been wronged and deserves retribution or pity (we'll look more into that in a later chapter).

In other words, prepare your mind and heart to tell your story from a *sacred and safe place*. In that way you will best reach the hearts of your readers.

What are some *wrong* reasons that might be motivating me to pen my memoir (and that I should be praying about)?

_____

_____

_____

_____

_____

_____

_____

_____

_____

_____

_____

_____

What are some *good* reasons that might be motivating me to pen my memoir?

_____

_____

_____

_____

_____

_____

_____

_____

_____

_____

_____

_____

_____

_____

_____

What type of person might be helped or inspired by my story?

_____

_____

_____

_____

_____

_____

_____

Write a prayer that asks God to help you specifically with these troubling feelings and motives so that you can tell an honest and inspiring story without getting in your own way:

_____

_____

_____

_____

_____

_____

_____

_____

_____

_____

_____

_____

_____

Writing Prompt:

"My ideal reader will be someone who . . ."

_____

_____

_____

_____

_____

_____

_____

_____

_____

_____

_____

_____

_____

Chapter 3: Important Considerations

When we tell our stories, we want to tell the truth. This can be challenging in three ways.

First, it can be painful to dig into our memories and hearts and face our fears and failures, yet being brutally honest is what will cause readers to not only empathize but draw inspiration and courage for their own situation.

Second, we don't want to hurt others who may be the culprits of pain in our stories.

Third, we don't want to open ourselves up to a lawsuit.

So how do you tell the truth yet protect your own heart and not end up with a libel suit for defaming someone? Or turning friends into enemies?

Protecting Yourself and Others

You may not have considered that writing about your life could be a dangerous endeavor. The degree of danger could vary from emotional distress to legal action to threats on your life. Hopefully, your story won't put you in anyone's crosshairs, but for some baring the truth, it has done just that.

But for most people beginning the journey of writing memoir, the greatest threat is to their own heart. And from their own heart.

As noted in the Introduction, a journey into the heart can open the door to pain, anger, hurt, and other emotions. This is why, first and foremost, every writing session should begin with prayer. Remember Philippians 4:6,7: "Be anxious for nothing." Through prayer and reliance on God to help you tell your story, "the peace of God . . . will protect your hearts and minds."

While it may be natural to shy away from reliving painful experiences, if you want readers to feel any intense emotions you felt as you went through those moments, you will have to dredge them up yourself and articulate them to faithfully convey them and help readers empathize with your experiences.

Here are three bits of advice on this matter:

- *Remind yourself that these are only memories*. They are void of power. They are like a shadow, not the substance, of past pain. You have already survived. You are already victorious. You control the story.

- *Keep readers safe by protecting them as they read.* How do you do that? By signaling early on, in various ways, that you are now okay. That what you went through may have been hard, yes, but you came out the other side and they can too. Inserting phrases such as "I did not yet know that after all that . . ." can help prepare readers for a possibly difficult read.

- Another way to protect your readers is by avoiding getting too graphic. That, of course, will be subjective, and sometimes the best way to know if we are giving too much detail about painful experiences is to bounce those chapters off of friends who are willing to read and give honest feedback.

Memoir or Novel?

If you feel you can't tell the whole truth in a way that will be impacting without causing trouble for those who played a part in your story, you might consider writing a fictional memoir or novel.

While this requires much study to learn how to structure such stories, it may be worthwhile to you to pursue in order to get your story and themes across.

I felt a clear leading from God to tell the story of my mother's betrayal of my family. It was a horrible time in my life, and it nearly destroyed my husband. I knew writing a memoir was out of the question—I feared violent retribution. (If we are writing about dangerous people, we have to take care to protect ourselves and our families).

I knew the take-home message my story was centered on this: that to live a healthy life, we sometimes have to cut toxic people out of our lives entirely—even if they are close family members. In my case, I had to distance my mother from me and my family. We moved hundreds of miles away to get out from under her influence. I also had to take legal action for protection.

Instead of writing a memoir, I decided to write a novel, but, as a novelist, this wasn't a daunting decision. As was recommended (by a lawyer-writer friend), to avoid trouble, I changed these three key elements of my story, and this might be something you'll want to do.

- The names of the "characters"

- The location in which the story is set

- The profession of the characters

Now that I was creating a novel, I added in fictional elements. *Conundrum* is 95% autobiographical and tells the story of a woman's attempt to solve the mystery of her father's death that occurred twenty-five years earlier, but in her attempt to do so, family lies and treachery are revealed that almost destroy her in her search for truth.

Almost every detail in the novel is true, drawn from my life. The inciting incident is my brother's attempt to kill himself, and that prompts "my character" to go on a search for answers to puzzling family mysteries.

The story ends at transformation, and though I turn it into a murder mystery (why not? No one ever discovered why my father died), the story is resolved at that point because of the character arc: Lisa has the courage to finally break free from her destructive mother, heals the breach in her relationship with her husband, and is on the road to healing and happiness, painful lessons learned.

Weigh the Risks

Writing your memoir may be risky in some way. When Shannon Hernandez wrote her memoir *Breaking the Silence: My Final Forty Days as a Public School Teacher* about her battle with the New York City Public Schools, she figured she would never get another job in that city again.

Yet, she also knew how important her story would be to the teachers, parents, and administrators in that school system, exposing the failures and negligence that was causing educators to leave the field in great numbers.

Through writing her story with brutal honesty, not only have readers responded enthusiastically, her book is bringing national attention to some of the problems with public education and shedding light on some awful things going on behind closed doors. She weighed the cost of candor.

Some stories need to be told, and while the telling may negatively impact us in some way, we feel compelled to tell it. Writing from a place of fear is never a good way to proceed. Our first obligation, should we forge ahead, is to the truth of our story, and that means not censoring ourselves.

As you begin to write, you may have two opposing voices in your head: the one that begs for the truth to be told and the other, the critic, warning you not to speak.

But no one is making you tell your story. Pray, take time to think it through. Count the cost. Even if you change names (and use a pen name), some people will know you wrote about them, casting them, perhaps, in a bad light, and they may never speak to you again.

Legal Ramifications

But let's take this a step further. Are there any legal implications when writing memoir? Can someone sue you for writing about them?

If you are in any doubt about the legal backwash should you tell your story, seek professional legal advice.

But here are some facts:

Memoir writers rarely get sued, and if they are, it's either for defamation of character or invasion of privacy.

Defamation is the claim that what you've written is untrue and that you are spreading lies *with malice*. If what you are writing is true (and maybe you can even back up the facts, if pressed), the person you've upset might be angry but won't be able to win a lawsuit against you.

You can't be sued for your opinion. Maybe your Aunt Sally doesn't like it that you portrayed her as a gossip and nag, but you're entitled to your opinion—even between the covers of a published book.

And because we all tend to color our memories a bit due to our emotions, placing a disclaimer on your copyright page might head off potential problems. You might say the events that are recorded in the book are those you remember to the best of your ability, though others may have a different take on those events. And that you mean no harm in anything you say.

An invasion of privacy lawsuit implies you are revealing things about a person that doesn't have legitimate "public concern." However, when you share experiences many people can relate to, this often justifies public concern or interest, and even gossip and smut—such as is said about some celebrities—can be (sadly) construed as justifiable public interest.

Again, this can be a tricky situation, so the best way to avoid potential lawsuits is to get permission first from the people you plan to write about. And if that isn't possible, as noted earlier, change enough details so that the person won't be easily recognized by her or those who know her.

Another way to avoid these pitfalls is to always couch your "claims" as opinions and not conclusions. There's a big difference between saying "My ex-husband was a drug dealer and made a fortune selling meth on the streets of San Jose" and "My guess was that my ex . . ." or "It appeared to me that my ex . . ." or "At the time I concluded that my ex . . . though I was never certain." Do you see the difference?

If you are going to tell a truthful memoir, then tell the truth. Don't embellish. Don't exaggerate. Don't use your memoir as therapy or a place to ramble about any old thought (that's what your journal is for).

You can't tell a powerful story if you're afraid of hurting people. As mentioned above, if you need to, change the names of people and places in your story. Tweak minor details to keep from exposing those who might be adversely affected by the things you write about them. But don't avoid diving into the bad, ugly, and hurtful.

Presenting Yourself Honestly

Avoid making yourself the superhero of your story. As with fiction, readers relate to real people. If you portray yourself as the hero in every situation—or the pathetic victim—you will turn off your readers.

You should come across human: with strengths and weaknesses, moments of vulnerability and courage. You should appear neither totally innocent nor totally guilty for the events that transpired. You aren't trying to appeal to everyone.

No one can be expected to remember the past perfectly. As you delve into your memory, you want to reconstruct as accurately as you can the events you want to share. Readers will recognize your honest attempt to be accurate. But they can also sense when a writer is lying or stretching the truth.

You may find that you are often speculating about things and drawing conclusions about motives, and when doing so, say so. Don't present those things as fact or blanket truth.

Memory is such a strange thing. It's not only personal, it's changeable. You may remember events quite differently at different times in your life. You may not recall what things happened at what dates. Don't stress about getting every little fact straight. Just do your best, without judgment.

For the sake of your story, you may move events around. You might embellish with details or dialogue that isn't exactly right but provides the gist of what was said. The point is to tell your story with integrity, capturing the essence as best as you are able.

The age-old question "What is truth" is pertinent here. Truth can be a matter of perspective. And, in the case of memoir, a matter of spotty memory.

Facing Your Fears

It can be painful to tell the truth. It can be painful to tell the facts of your story as well as share the emotional content.

It can be scary to release your story into the world with its possible resultant self-exposure, embarrassment, risk of retaliation or backlash, loss of privacy, loss of your job, loss of close family and/or friends, and ostracism.

Sometimes friends, coworkers, or family members threaten us and warn us not to tell our story.

Telling the truth sometimes breaks spoken or unspoken rules, for within community it is often expected that "what happens here, stays here."

When Alice Walker wrote about black men abusing black women in *The Color Purple*, even though the book was fiction, she was publicly attacked for betraying the black community.

We may find that even our innocuous, humorous story might ruffle the feathers of some who feel they are being made fun of or maligned.

So why risk all this? You probably already know the answer. Not only do you feel led to tell your story; there are others who may need to hear it. Others need you to tell the truth. And that's good to remember when you are experiencing fear or doubt.

The sense of shared humanity is an important part of culture, and when we share stories, we feel a little less alone in the world. Alice Walker said, "When I write about my family, about things from the South, the people of China say, 'Why, this is very Chinese.'"

Some of your experiences may feel too difficult to share. Maybe they are utterly embarrassing to even think of. No one is holding a gun to your head and forcing you to share everything painful in your past or go into gory or graphic detail.

But if you believe it's important to share these kinds of experiences, then overcoming your own inhibitions is going to be challenging. What you consider taboo is often something many others do as well. How can you write about these events in a style or voice that won't alienate readers?

Who might be offended or hurt in some way by my story and why?

_____

_____

_____

_____

_____

_____

_____

_____

_____

_____

_____

_____

_____

What are some of my deep fears about telling the truth of my story?
What is the worst that might happen, and can I live with that?

_____

_____

_____

_____

_____

_____

_____

_____

_____

_____

_____

What are some details about my story that I could possibly leave out in
order to spare someone (or myself) undue pain?

_____

_____

_____

_____

_____

_____

_____

_____

_____

_____

Writing Prompt:

"If I wasn't so afraid, I would tell you about the time when . . ."

_____

_____

_____

_____

_____

_____

_____

_____

_____

_____

_____

_____

_____

_____

Chapter 4: Structuring a Memoir

There are countless ways you might structure your memoir, so give this some thought. Consider what your theme is, the collection of memories you want to write about, and where you want to it to end.

Here are a few different structures for memoirs:

- **Linear:** The most straightforward memoirs are those that start at point A and end at point B, moving the reader along in linear time. These include coming-of-age memoirs, such as Augusten Burroughs's *Running with Scissors* and Julia Scheeres's *Jesus Land*, or books that take place over the course of a year, such as Julia Powell's *Julie and Julia: 365 Days, 524 Recipes, 1 Tiny Apartment Kitchen*.

  A linear structure may have more than one timeline. You could recount a past period of time and alternate with a more current time period. This is beautifully done in Sarah Thebarge's memoir *The Invisible Girls*. (See the back of this workbook for the chapter-by-chapter breakdown of this structure.)

- **Framed:** Consider Cheryl Strayed's *Wild: From Lost to Found on the Pacific Crest Trail*, whose narrative is contained over the five-month period of her hike and yet includes flashbacks to her childhood, her upbringing, past relationships, and what brought her to the current timeline of the narrative. The story follows a timeline but also jumps back to incidents that are topical for a given chapter.

- **Thematic:** Lucy Grealey's *Autobiography of a Face* spans a twenty-year period, with a timeline that is neither linear nor framed but is clearly focused on a singular issue: deformity and its impact on the author.

- **Creative**: Your story may be perfect for an unusual structure. Author Jesmyn Ward begins her memoir, *Men We Reaped*, with the death of her younger brother. From there she tells the story forward from her birth as well as backward from the death of the fifth man in her account, and the two timelines intersect at the end of the book with that younger brother's death. The purpose of the memoir is tied up with these five deaths.

What kind of memoir might be the best for your story and why?

_____

_____

_____

_____

_____

_____

_____

_____

Try to explain in a couple of sentences the overall storyline (pretend this is your back cover copy on your book):

_____

_____

_____

_____

_____

_____

_____

_____

Make a list of the ten or so key moments you will highlight in your memoir (a brief phrase or sentence for each). Set them out as they come to you, in random order:

_____

_____

_____

_____

_____

_____

_____

_____

_____

_____

_____

_____

Now put them in order of when they occurred:

_____

_____

_____

_____

_____

_____

_____

_____

_____

_____

_____

_____

Play around with a different order. See if this organization feels more appropriate than a linear timeline.

_____

_____

_____

_____

_____

_____

_____

_____

_____

_____

What conclusion have you come to regarding the best way to structure your memoir?

_____

_____

_____

_____

"Don't make the mistake of thinking it is easier to tell the stories you have lived than to make up fictitious stories about imaginary people. It is no easier to write your own story well than it is to write anything else well."

— _Writing the Memoir_, Judith Barrington

Chapter 5: Theme at the Heart of Your Story

What is theme? Merriam-Webster's Dictionary gives this as one of the definitions: a specific and distinctive quality, characteristic, or concern.

Your memoir *concerns* something. You may not yet know what that *something* is, but with some thought and self-examination, you should be able to come up with a theme or perhaps multiple themes for your memoir.

Why is this important? As mentioned earlier, it speaks to your purpose, why you are writing your story. Perhaps, as Maya Angelou did, you want to share with readers the milieu of your childhood and the culture in which you were raised, with the intention of shedding light on issues that *concerned* you or others around you.

While you don't necessarily need to have a huge or narrow theme, such as overcoming addiction, a fertility struggle, or surviving a bad or abusive relationship, you do need to have a "point" to writing your story. Even one that is funny and meant to entertain—perhaps an account of a wild experience—will have a theme at its heart. So spend some time thinking about that theme.

Theme Is the Glue That Holds Your Story Together

Your theme should infuse every chapter you write, whether strong in the forefront or subtle in the background. With every chapter, you must always keep sight of it. It's the thread that weaves through your entire book and ties all the chapters together. It's the glue that binds.

Again, studying great memoirs that are similar to what you want to write will help. Find three, at least, and mark them up with a highlighter. Make a list of the chapters and summarize what each chapter covers. And especially highlight every time the theme(s) is referenced in some way.

This is how you will keep on track so you don't ramble or include incidents in your life that are unrelated. If readers are reading because they want to see how you dealt with something specific, if you include chapters about events in your life that *don't serve the purpose of your story*, they will get confused, annoyed, and possibly lose interest.

Memoirs with themes have the strongest draw in the "memoir" category because readers are drawn to stories they can relate to. When we bring universal themes into our memoir, we cast a wide net that will "catch" readers in many places and from many walks of life.

Take a look at this passage from Elizabeth Gilbert's *Eat, Pray, Love*:

> But is it such a bad thing to live like this for just a little while? Just for a few months of one's life, is it so awful to travel through time with no greater ambition than to find the next lovely meal? Or to learn how to speak a language for no higher purpose than that it pleases your ear to hear it? Or to nap in a garden, in a patch of sunlight, in the middle of the day, right next to your favorite foundation? And then to do it again the next day?
>
> Of course, no one can live like this forever.

Gilbert is stopping to consider the life she's living. She's reflecting on her journey, and if you do this periodically throughout your story, you will drive home the theme that you want your reader to get and resonate with.

Donald Miller, in his best-selling memoir *Blue Like Jazz*, writes:

> I didn't like being reminded about how self-absorbed I was. . . . I didn't want to live in a broken world or a broken me. . . .
>
> I know now, from experience, that the path to joy winds through this dark valley. I think every well-adjusted human being has dealt squarely with his or her own depravity. . . . Nothing is going to change in the Congo until you and I figure out what is wrong with the person in the mirror.

Issa Rae writes this in her introduction, and the stories that she shares are all about her theme:

> I'm coming clean with all the awkward, the embarrassing, the disappointing, the frustrating moments that have made me, many of which have turned out to be teaching moments . . .
>
> Whether you're an awkward black girl or a confident white guy, my hope is that you'll learn from my mistakes and, at the very least, laugh at my misgivings.

One way to think about theme is to consider the lessons you've learned through your journey: about life, about yourself, about the world.

What you've learned through your journey equates to the gems you'll want to share in your memoir.

What important lessons have you learned from your experiences that you want to convey in your memoir?

_____

_____

_____

_____

_____

_____

_____

_____

_____

_____

_____

_____

Make a list of three notable moments in your life when you learned one of these key lessons. What incidents come to mind and why are they notable?

_____

_____

_____

_____

_____

_____

_____

_____

_____

_____

_____

_____

_____

_____

_____

Picking a Title

Maybe you've been considering a title for your memoir. Bringing themes into your title and using quotations can pound home your themes. Take a look at Sarah Thebarge's memoir *The Invisible Girls.*

Hers is the story of how, after nearly dying of breast cancer in her twenties, Sarah fled her successful career and moved three thousand miles away to find solace and to pick up the pieces of her broken life. On the train home from work shortly after moving to Portland, she met a family of Somali refugees that swept her into an adventure that changed all their lives.

Sarah opens the memoir with this quote by Ralph Ellison, author of the highly acclaimed novel *The Invisible Man*, who wrote about the invisibility of being African American in the first half of the twentieth century: "I am invisible, understand, simply because people refuse to see me."

Sarah used the theme of invisibility as the framework for her story.

Jesmyn Ward's memoir, *Men We Reaped*, is centered on the deaths of five young black men. She quotes Harriet Tubman at the beginning of her story:

> We saw the lightning and that was the guns; and then we heard the thunder and that was the big gun; and then we heard the rain falling and that was the blood falling; and when we came to get in the crops, it was dead men that we reaped.

Kimberly Rae Miller's memoir *Coming Clean* documents her life living with her father, who was a hoarder. Perhaps an odd theme to center a memoir on, her book looks deep into places we call home and our relationships with our parents. Note how her clever title emphasizes her theme.

If your story is one off adventure or giving insight into the daily life experience of a particular career, your title might best embody that focus.

Titles such as *With Byrd at the Bottom of the World* (Norman D. Vaughan), an account by a man who went on the South Pole expedition of 1928; *Within Arm's Length* (Dan Emmett), the story of a Secret Service agent; and *On the Road with Janis Joplin* (John Byrne Cooke) signal a potential reader right away what the memoir will be about.

The Mountain: My Time on Everest (Ed Viesturs) implies risk, danger, and a gripping tale. Usually, a descriptive title in this vein is all that's needed to get across the purpose of the story and its potential themes.

Write what comes to mind when you read each of the following words: a memory, a thought, a way this word ties in with your story.

Disappointment:

_____

_____

_____

Accomplishment:

_____

_____

_____

Victory:

_____

_____

_____

Fear:

_____

_____

_____

Gratitude:

_____

_____

_____

Which of those words, memories, or thoughts feel closest to the heart of your story? Why?

_____

_____

_____

_____

_____

_____

_____

_____

_____

Make a list of other words that spring into your mind that embody the theme or purpose of your story:

_____

_____

_____

_____

_____

_____

_____

_____

_____

_____

_____

_____

Play around with titles for your memoir that include some of those words, to emphasize your possible theme:

_____

_____

_____

_____

_____

_____

_____

_____

_____

_____

_____

Can you narrow down that list of words to maybe three that showcase your theme? How about one word? How might that one word embody your memoir?

_____

_____

_____

_____

_____

_____

_____

_____

_____

_____

Try crafting that one word into a statement or phrase:

_____

_____

_____

_____

_____

If your memoir is more "event" or "career" focused, play around with some possible titles that clearly reflect that:

_____

_____

_____

_____

_____

_____

_____

_____

_____

"Eric and I could probably have gotten to the summit on May 21. But I'm not sure I'd be here to tell about it today. For all the remorse that turning back so close to the top flooded me with in the months and years after our attempt, I can see in retrospect that it was one of the best decisions I've made in my life . . . That near miss in 1987 was the first vivid demonstration of a moral I would come to live by as I pursued all fourteen 8,000ers: _Listen to the mountain. You can always come back. It will still be there._"

— _The Mountain: My Time on Everest_, Ed Viesturs

Writing Prompt:

"What I did not know about myself then was . . ."

_____

_____

_____

_____

_____

_____

_____

_____

_____

_____

_____

_____

_____

_____

What to Avoid When Writing Your Memoir

- *Don't get preachy.* You may be excited about your themes, and that can be a pitfall—because when we're excited, we can get preachy. And we don't want our memoirs to be like a sermon. Instead of lecturing your reader, think how you can let the experiences speak for themselves. Remember: actions speak louder than words.

- *Watch out that your memoir isn't a channel for venting your anger or hurt at someone.* Venting can be healing, but readers don't want to hear you rant.

- *Consider changing names* if you are going to show the gory or sordid details of close family members, friends, or coworkers.

- *Avoid a tone that will turn off readers.* If you brag, condescend, show an angry or cynical attitude (because you are hurting or are feeling vengeful), you are going to upset readers. If you need to vent, do so in your journal or in the shower where no one but God will hear you.

- *Don't get locked into a narrow focus.* The tendency may be just to tell about yourself and your experience, but you'll need to bring in other "characters" and outside elements that affected you: locale, neighbors, community, family, coworkers, friends. Think how you might show these impacting and informing your experiences.

- *Don't just tell: show.* Don't just say that you went to Africa—show what it felt and smelled and sounded like. Describe the sensory details to immerse your reader fully in your story.

- *Don't wander off into unrelated material.* It's tempting to share incidents or anecdotes from your life that you feel are meaningful or amusing or impacting. But many of those valued accounts have no place in the specific story you intend to tell. Be intentional and stay focused. Don't "show boring home movies" to your readers!

Part 2: Beginning to Write Your Book

Chapter 6: How to Determine a Starting Point

Your memoir obviously needs to start somewhere and end somewhere, and since you're not writing an autobiography with the purpose of detailing your entire life, you need to spend time thinking about the time frame.

One writer suggests: "Start anywhere. Because no matter where you start, you'll end up where you're meant to be." I disagree. From my experience in critiquing and editing hundreds of manuscripts, including memoir, if you start anywhere, you may wander off to Shangri-la and find yourself stuck in a snowdrift—not where you'd planned to go.

As with any journey, you need a specific starting point that will actually get you to your targeted destination.

Your memoir may cover three days of your life or it may cover thirty years. You could be writing a gripping story of the time you got trapped in a hotel during a tsunami or the year you spent living abroad. The duration is contingent on the particular story you aim to tell.

This is why it's important to know your purpose in writing this particular memoir and your themes.

Since your memoir is going to pull from various anecdotes in your life to support your theme or topic, you want to determine what event in your life is best to springboard your story.

Let's look at a few different methods:

- You might start off your memoir with that key, powerful event in your life that sets the stage for your story, but from there, *you may want to skip ahead in time* (even years) to when that event starting impacting you in a specific way.

  For instance, let's say you experienced some traumatic event in your childhood—think of Maya Angelou's incident at age eight (telling someone about the man who raped her, who then was

44

murdered) that left her mute for years. You may decide to open your memoir with that event, playing it out like a movie scene so readers see what germinated the events to follow.

From there you might begin your actual memoir decades later, when you fall in love with the man you will marry. That "inciting incident"—as is called in novel structure—is what begins the bigger story that highlights your themes.

Maybe it's when you marry that the submerged memories of your abuse start surfacing. Or you discover fears and roadblocks to happiness in your marriage because you haven't dealt with that past pain.

- Or you might start right in with your "inciting incident." If your story is about how you got sucked into drug addiction, you might begin with the day you met that attractive man who took you to that party and got you so drunk, you didn't realize you had been given meth or cocaine or some other drug. From there, things start going downhill.

Consider Joan Didion's memoir, *The Year of Magical Thinking.* The memoir begins with her husband's death, which launched the tumultuous and life-changing year that followed.

- If your story is meant to show how far you've come in life in some specific way, you might start by showing your previous life or situation just before things change.

Consider *The Pursuit of Happyness*, which starts by showing Chris Gardner investing all his savings into buying machines to sell, which leads him to becoming broke and losing his wife. Though things look hopeless, he is determined to rise up and succeed, and shortly thereafter learns of a possible position as a stockbroker. The odds are against him, but even though he is homeless and taking care of his young son, he works hard and applies himself, then lands the coveted job.

You might start at the point that shows how bad things once were for you. From there, you would share *the pivotal experiences* in your life, the important people who aided in your transformation, what you learned, and how you applied certain principles to arrive at the place where you were victorious.

Think about your "moment of discovery" or an iconic incident that highlights your theme. This is the key moment when your specific story began. Think to that point in the past when your life started to shift.

Jot down some thoughts about that moment. Where were you? What was going on in your life? How did you feel?

_____

_____

_____

_____

_____

_____

_____

_____

_____

_____

_____

_____

_____

_____

Take a look at how Abigail Thomas begins with her moment of discovery:

Monday, April 24, at nine forty at night, our doorman Pedro called me on the intercom. "Your dog is in the elevator," he said. The world had just changed forever, and I think I knew it even then.

Abigail learned that night that her husband, who had been out walking their dog, got hit by a car. Her story about her husband's slow and difficult recovery from traumatic brain injury then begins.

The accident was her "inciting incident" for her story.

Can you describe your key event as if it were a movie scene? Give it a try:

_____

_____

_____

_____

_____

_____

_____

_____

_____

_____

_____

Endings

Talking about beginnings brings us to this pertinent question: Where will your memoir end?

Just as your memoir doesn't start at your birth, it shouldn't end at the end of your life. It may end at the moment you are in right now, but only if that is the natural "culmination" of your story.

What does that mean?

Think again of the purpose or themes of your memoir. Just as you had a moment of discovery, an inciting incident that set your story in motion, you also have a moment in which you have "arrived."

That doesn't mean you aren't continuing to learn and grow from what you went through, but you should end your story at the place where the lessons have hit home. When you've taken those epiphanies you've gleaned from your experiences and now use them to light the way forward.

Whether you have taken visible action steps because of the lessons learned, or you've made new plans, or you've changed your outlook or beliefs—any or all of those might signal the perfect place to end your story.

The ending for your particular story may be obvious. It could be when you left your job for good (quit or retired or were fired). When you ran across the (literal or figurative) finish line and reached your goal.

Leaving Your Readers with a Strong Sense of Conclusion

It's best, once the "goal" has been reached, to end the book and not go off on new tangents or other journeys. The reader has joined with you on this journey, and when you get to "the end," there should be a sense of completion, reflection, and resolution. Just as with a great novel, the ending should satisfyingly "wrap up" the story and any loose ends.

You may want to skip ahead in time, perhaps many years, to conclude your story and wrap things up for your readers long after the "period" your memoir covers ended.

Norman Vaughan went to the South Pole with Admiral Byrd 1928-1930, but he ends his memoir by jumping ahead to 1957, when Byrd dies and he is at his commander's graveside. He beautifully plays out this moment to give readers a feeling of completion and emotional satisfaction.

Byrd's funeral was spectacular, with many VIPs in attendance. . . . The taps blown at the graveside brought tears to my eyes. I made no attempt to wipe them away, and I didn't care if anyone else noticed. I was saying good-bye to a great man.

I stood at attention, listening to taps while vivid memories flashed through my mind. I thought of my first meeting with Byrd at Wonalancet, when he inspected the dogs . . . my carrying him by sled to Little America . . . our walks along the barrier in Antarctica . . . his phone calls and letters . . . his parting words when he left for his second expedition, back to Antarctica . . . In my mind I saw him again on the frozen continent as we hastened to board the battered *City* in the Bay of Whales after our year at the bottom of the world.

"It's over, Norman," he had said. The smile—I saw the smile again, too. "We did it."

Yes, I thought. *We did it.*

Note how Vaughan brings his title, *With Byrd at the Bottom of the World*, into play in the last lines of his memoir. That, too, helps give readers a feeling of completion, driving home the focus and purpose of the memoir.

Think about those lessons you learned by the end of your journey—how what you went through changed you.

What was the defining moment when your lessons finally manifested in a change, decision, or new outlook? Describe that moment or incident:

_____

_____

_____

_____

_____

_____

_____

_____

_____

_____

_____

_____

_____

_____

_____

What sense of resolution or conclusions will you come to (or lead the reader to) at the end of your memoir?

_____

_____

_____

_____

_____

_____

_____

_____

What specific event "wraps up" your story at the end in a natural and satisfying way?

_____

_____

_____

_____

_____

_____

_____

_____

_____

_____

_____

_____

Does this help you clarify a framework of time for your memoir?

Whatever structure you use, the starting point and ending point need to be firmly fixed in your mind so that your story takes place between the two moments.

You may flash back to earlier or later times, but those will be side dishes to your main story, helping support your themes.

Think about not just the events in that ending moment but also how this ending point might be a satisfying conclusion of your story.

How Long Should My Memoir Be?

You may be wondering how to determine the ideal length for your memoir. While there are no hard-and-fast rules, most full-length books are between 60,000 and 80,000 words. If you write under 30,000 words, you are writing more of a short story than a book.

Maybe all you want to do is write a brief account—an article or story. That's perfectly fine. If you have no interest in writing a book, or the idea of a big project is intimidating, don't pressure yourself.

Tell the story you want to tell. If it's long and deep, chances are it will evolve into a full-length book. Don't worry about word or page count; that will only distract or aggravate you. Focus on the craft of storytelling.

Writing Prompt:

"If only someone had told me when I was young that . . ."

_____

_____

_____

_____

_____

_____

_____

_____

_____

_____

_____

_____

Chapter 7: Putting Your Memories in Order

Before you begin writing your memoir, think about the events that are most relevant and distinct in your memory in relation to your overarching theme. Make these events your focus.

For now, don't think about the structure you've chosen. The first steps require that you come up with enough incidents in your life that support your theme and show your character arc—those things that affected and changed you.

Remember the elephant: one bite at a time.

Have you already come up with that starting point, the "inciting incident"? If so, write a brief description here:

_____

_____

_____

_____

_____

Now, make a list of 10-15 key incidents that occurred during the time frame of your memoir that will build your story, one sentence or phrase per incident:

_____

_____

_____

_____

_____

_____

_____

_____

_____

_____

_____

_____

_____

_____

_____

_____

How might you link all these incidents together? What is the thread that runs through them all? Pick two of the scenes you listed and brainstorm what links them together:

_____

_____

_____

_____

_____

_____

_____

_____

_____

_____

_____

Spend some time, on your computer or pad or paper, playing with the themes and topics and issues that might serve as a way to connect all your story pieces together.

If some incident doesn't seem to fit at all (maybe it's a significant or funny event in your life, so you really want to share it), consider leaving it out. Every moment you include in your story should serve the purpose of the memoir. It should shed light on the specific premise your memoir is shaped around. It's hard to force a square-shaped memory into a round-shaped memoir!

Get the Ideas Flowing!

Write about one moment when you gave up or almost did:

_____

_____

_____

_____

_____

_____

_____

_____

_____

_____

_____

_____

_____

Write about one moment when someone gave you advice, strength, or help that got you through:

_____

_____

_____

_____

_____

_____

_____

_____

_____

_____

_____

Write about one moment of stark realization about yourself that shook your world:

_____

_____

_____

_____

_____

_____

_____

_____

_____

_____

_____

_____

_____

Write about one moment when you felt a special sense of victory or accomplishment:

_____

_____

_____

_____

_____

_____

_____

_____

_____

_____

_____

_____

_____

_____

Traditional Story Structure

Think about applying traditional story structure that is utilized in fiction. Here are the primary developments in order:

- Setup. Showing your "character" in her world at the start of the story

- Inciting incident or "opportunity" arises shortly after (this can be in your opening scene)

- Followed by efforts to deal with, rise above, fight, or adapt to the new situation

- Followed by setbacks, complications, greater obstacles and challenges, all with a particular goal or objective in mind (to get free, to find someone or something, to deliver something, to win, etc.)

- The dark night moment or backsliding or hopelessness before the big climax, which is where the goal is reached (victory or defeat)

- The resolution of the story, showing the growth, change, lessons learned

Take some time to think about all of these various stages. As you begin writing or do further brainstorming, no doubt you will come up with many more "scenes" or situations that will fit into these sections or fill the gaps between them.

Try coming up with some ideas to start.

Setup. Where am I at the start of my story and why? What am I doing? What is my living situation? What relationships are in play?

_____

_____

_____

_____

_____

_____

_____

_____

_____

_____

_____

_____

Inciting Incident (You've already worked on this, so try to add details):

_____

_____

_____

_____

_____

_____

_____

_____

_____

List some of the obstacles, setbacks, disappointments, betrayals, or twists that come into your play in your story:

_____

_____

_____

_____

_____

_____

_____

Talk about the greatest dark moments, hardest challenge, or overwhelming obstacles you have to face and push through right before your story culminates:

_____

_____

_____

_____

_____

_____

_____

_____

_____

_____

How does your situation change by the end and in what way so that you bring a satisfying and insightful wrap-up to your memoir?

_____

_____

_____

_____

_____

_____

_____

_____

_____

_____

_____

Because it's so easy to drift off into events and topics that aren't tied into your theme or the purpose of your memoir, it helps to make some firm decisions on the parameters of your story. In other words, what you will omit.

List some of the things you have chosen not to include in your memoir:

_____

_____

_____

_____

_____

_____

_____

_____

_____

_____

This will help you keep on track, stay focused on the purpose of your memoir, and avoid adding in material that is inconsequential or unrelated.

"Without my mother's legacy, I would never have been able to look at this history of loss, this future where I will surely lose more, and write the narrative that remembers, write the narrative that says: _Hello. We are here. Listen._ It is not easy. I continue. Sometimes I am tireless. And sometimes I am weary."

— _Men We Reaped_, Jesmyn Ward

Chapter 8: Writing Nuts and Bolts

There is so much involved in learning how to write well and tell a powerful, engaging story, and this workbook can only scratch the surface of this vast topic. Consider getting books on grammar, writing composition, and other related writing subjects. Take some classes on composition or creative writing at a local college. Attend writing workshops and join a MeetUp group in your area so you can get great advice, encouragement, and critiques. Or hire a writing coach for more pointed and personal assistance with your memoir.

We do need to take a look at a few issues of writing craft at this juncture because you have some decisions to make.

All your events in your memoir took place in the past, before this very moment. But that doesn't necessarily mean you must write your book in past tense.

What Tense Should You Write In?

The tenses used in memoir are past tense and present tense (some writers use both).

It may be easier to tell your story when you imagine it happening *now*, in the "now of your story," but many find writing in present tense difficult. You may want to try writing in both present and past tense to see which you prefer.

Present tense often feels more immediate and personal. And that might perfectly suit you. Take a look at some passages from memoirs written in present tense:

> Sweat drips into my eyes, warping the landscape, and I lift my T-shirt to wipe my face, flashing my bra at the empty world. Ahead of me, David rides shirtless, his scrawny torso gleaming like melting

chocolate. . . . If anyone from Harrison sees us, we're doomed. (*Jesus Land*, Julia Scheeres)

I arrive in Paris on September 12, 1988, armed with two Polaroid pictures and three years of high school French. I am eighteen, straight out of Catholic school, and about to discover what it's like to be one of the 99 percent of international fashion models who never make it onto the cover of *Vogue*. (*Runway: Confessions of a Not-So-Supermodel*, Meghan Ward)

When I think of a stranger touching my daughter's clothes it feels like a violation, so donating them to Goodwill is out of the questions. But then several months after the funeral, one of her cousins asks if she can have Maya's prettiest formal dress. I examine the dress, opulent as a peony, its hot pink bodice and spaghetti straps, the skirt with its cascade of pink flounces. . . . [I[wrap the dress in tissue paper . . . and present it to my niece. (*Swimming with Maya: A Mother's Story*, Eleanor Vincent)

Try writing about a past event in present tense. If you need a prompt, try starting with "The moment I walk into the room, I see . . ."

_____

_____

_____

_____

_____

_____

_____

_____

_____

_____

How did that feel? Keep in mind that while you might write your story in present tense, anytime you reflect further back in the past, you may need to use past tense.

If you write "I am riding on the carousel at the county fair," and then you think about the first time you rode one, you would word it like this: "As my pony is moving up and down, I think about the first time my mother put me on a carousel. I was terrified and cried, but she merely smiled and waved at me as I went by."

The Now of Your Story

The reason you may need to switch tenses is because there is a "now" of your story, and there is everything before that. The above example uses present tense for "the now" and past tense for prior events.

If you decide to write your memoir in past tense, you will need to take care to be clear what events are happening in your "now" and which were earlier.

For example, see how the distinction is made between the "now" of this passage and prior events:

> I drove my car down to the seaside. When I parked and got out, I watched the waves break on the shore. Years ago, when I used to come here as a child, I would stand at the water's edge and dare the waves to get me. Now, as I walked up to the water, I wished those same waves would engulf me.

Here is the same passage written using present tense for the "now" of the story:

> I drive my car down to the seaside. When I park and get out, I watch the waves break on the shore. Years ago, when I used to come here as a child, I would stand at the water's edge and dare the waves to get me. Now, as I walk up to the water, I wish those same waves would engulf me.

As you can see, there's not much difference between the two, and you can clearly see the difference between the "now" and the past.

Not to confuse you, but some writers pen their memoir in past tense for the "now" of their story and use present tense for prior events. Take a look at this rewrite of the above passage:

> I drove my car down to the seaside. When I parked and got out, I watched the waves break on the shore. *I am five years old, standing at the water's edge, taunting the waves to come drench me, my laughter filling the air. I am invincible; nothing can harm me.* Now, as I walked up to the water, I wished those same waves would engulf me. I was not invincible any longer. I was riddled with the bullet holes of betrayal and failure.

As you can see, there are many ways to use the various tenses to good effect. If you don't have a lot of writing experience, I would suggest keeping it simple and in the tense(s) that feel most natural for you.

Rewrite the passage you just wrote into past tense:

_____

_____

_____

_____

_____

_____

_____

_____

_____

_____

Writing Prompt:

"The deepest moral dilemma of my life was when . . ."

_____

_____

_____

_____

_____

_____

_____

_____

_____

_____

_____

_____

_____

Chapter 9: Tone and Voice

Voice is like your fingerprint. Each of us has a voice when we speak aloud. We have a style of speaking, our own unique vocabulary and syntax and inflections.

When we write, we also adopt a "voice." We can (and should) carefully choose the type of voice that permeates our memoir.

Voice is different from tone, but the two are connected. If you plan to write a humorous memoir, the tone will be funny and light (though you can have dark humor too), and the voice you would use would need to fit that tone.

Your story may be one of very painful, dark, and/or terrifying experiences. But that does not mean your tone should be dark, nor that your voice should be heavy, somber, depressing.

The tone of your memoir might be serious, lighthearted, angry, sad, thoughtful—or the tone may vary throughout the telling. But avoid sounding whiny or looking for sympathy. Readers will naturally sympathize with your story if you present it in a way that doesn't annoy them.

Author Diane Johnson said, "Pain plus time equals comedy." That doesn't mean that we will find the hurts or abuse or suffering we went through as humorous. What it implies is that distance gives perspective and, well, distance. We need to have sufficient distance in order to tell a mature story.

This is very important to ponder.

If your memoir is to be a serious account that reveals a lot of pain, hurt, abuse, or other "heavy" incidents, keeping in mind *why* you are writing your story and *for whom* will help frame the question: What voice and tone do I want to use?

Heavy, painful subjects, of course, shouldn't be made light of. Or should they? Humor can take the edge off serious topics so that they are approachable.

Earlier you explored these questions, and we looked at how memoir is not a journal in which we rant or vent. It's not a means to inflict vengeance or pay back to those who've hurt you. If you need to rant, work through your pain, deal with your anger, that's what your journal and prayer (and possibly counseling) is for. If you feel you are unable to "distance" yourself from those feelings, you may not be ready for memoir-writing.

Remember: you are bearing witness, not wallowing.

Getting Readers to Care

To get readers enrapt in your story and caring about what happened in your life, your voice needs to be engaging, clear and concise, and conversational. You aren't writing a textbook or a doctoral thesis.

Imagine yourself sitting with a friend at your kitchen table, just chatting and sharing stories. If it helps, picture that friend (pick one who's a good listener and nonjudgmental! Or make up your ideal friend) as you write the chapters of your memoir, anticipating the questions she might ask and what details she'd want to know. Maybe even the funny or poignant remarks she'd make, which could really be your own insights into your past.

When you write your memoir, the reader should feel *spoken to.* Not lectured but included. By studying great memoirs, you can see how various authors do this.

The Self as Narrator

Yes, your story is about you, but it helps to separate yourself as the protagonist or main character of your story and the "you" that is the author.

Doing this helps give you perspective and distance, which is needed to craft your memoir. Can you picture yourself standing on a hill or across the street, watching what is happening to you in a particular "scene" you want to write about?

Let's try that.

Picture a key moment in your memoir. Imagine yourself standing one hundred yards away, watching the scene unfold. Imagine you are just an observer, someone else who witnesses without judgment. Write what you see:

_____

_____

_____

_____

_____

_____

_____

_____

_____

_____

_____

_____

Of course, we don't want our memoir to be straight facts without commentary, emotion, or elaboration. That would drain all the power out of our story. We do need to evoke emotion, but how do we do it without getting all emotional ourselves in our narrative?

Here is where the mature self comes into play.

The Mature Self

Ah, this is the secret at the crux of great memoir. We have to write our story, the events of our life, from a future perspective. From *now*.

Now brings with it maturity, wisdom, insight, and grace. The mature self speaks from that place of distance but not detachment.

This will take some thoughtful effort and time. Before you write any scene or chapter, you have to consider what you've learned, what perspective you want to offer on the situation. You have to accurately convey what you were feeling at the time without expressing those feelings *now*.

Take a look at this example from Maya Angelou's *I Know Why the Caged Bird Sings*. Here she is listening to the radio with a crowd gathered in her grandmother's store--the fight between Joe Louis and Primo Carnera, as the announcer declares Louis seems about to lose:

> My race groaned. It was our people falling. It was another lynching, yet another Black man hanging on a tree. One more woman ambushed and raped. A Black boy whipped and maimed. It was hounds on the trail of a man running through slimy swamps. It was a white woman slapping her maid for being forgetful.
> . . . This might be the end of the world. If Joe lost, we were back in slavery and beyond help. It would all be true, the accusations that we were lower types of human beings. Only a little higher than the apes. True that we were stupid and ugly and lazy and dirty and, unlucky and worst of all, that God Himself hated us and ordained us to be hewers of wood and drawers of water, forever and ever, world without end.
> We didn't breathe. We didn't hope. We waited.

Notice that Angelou doesn't rant here. She is sharing the perspective of herself and her people in a powerful way, as the mature narrator. Sure, you can reenact scenes showing yourself emotional *then*—angry, raging, crying—but that's something different from narrative voice, the mature self that is documenting the events like a historian.

You may choose to add in emotional commentary, in the present or *now* as you share those past events. But, again, you want to be careful.

Perhaps the most beautifully crafted and "careful" (think: full of care) passage of Angelou's entire memoir is when she describes being raped by her mother's husband at age eight.

> He released me enough to snatch down my bloomers, and then he dragged me closer to him. Turning the radio up loud, too loud, he said, "If you scream, I'm gonna kill you. And if you tell, I'm gonna kill Bailey." I could tell he meant what he said. I couldn't understand why he wanted to kill my brother. Neither of us had done anything to him. And then.
>
> Then there was the pain. A breaking and entering when even the senses are torn apart. The act of rape on an eight-year-old body is a matter of the needle giving because the camel can't. The child gives, because the body can, and the mind of the violator cannot.
>
> I thought I had died—I woke up in a white-walled world, and it had to be heaven. But Mr. Freeman [her rapist] was there and he was washing me. His hands shook, but he held me upright in the tub and washed my legs. "I didn't mean to hurt you, Ritie. I didn't mean it. But don't you tell . . . Remember, don't you tell a soul."

Surely, she could have gone into much greater detail, and attached (rightly so) much emotion to this horrific incident. But by speaking from a distanced, almost detached, mature self, she brings that power and grace to the moment that is too horrible to imagine. In a way, she protects or insulates her readers without minimizing the account. Still, it's heartbreaking.

That takes some thoughtful writing. She is telling the truth in a way that makes it easy for readers to read. As we discussed earlier, we want to be careful to protect our readers by our choice of words and depth of description. This is, also, where the mature self comes into play.

But Angelou wrote: "Easy reading is damn hard writing. I am trying to tell the truth, not everything I know, but the truth."

71

Tell the truth, but "not everything you know." Filter your experience through the eyes and mind of your mature self. Step back and leave your anger curbside.

I like what author Toni Morrison says about avoiding writing from a place of anger:

> Anger . . . it's a paralyzing emotion . . . you can't get anything done. People sort of think it's an interesting, passionate, and igniting feeling—I don't think it's any of that—it's helpless . . . it's absence of control—and I need all of my skills, all of the control, all of my powers . . . and anger doesn't provide any of that—I have no use for it whatsoever.

The mature self tells the truth, but truth isn't the same as facts. Truth is something deeper.

Morrison also says: "The crucial distinction for me is not the difference between fact and fiction but the distinction between fact and truth. Because facts can exist without human intelligence but truth cannot."

Consider that brief scene you wrote earlier (p. 65)—the one devoid of emotion. Now try to rewrite that scene adding in the truths you want to share with the reader—the truths your mature self knows well and wants the reader to understand:

_____

_____

_____

_____

_____

_____

_____

_____

_____

_____

_____

_____

_____

_____

_____

_____

_____

_____

_____

_____

Speaking Directly to Your Reader

Think about whether you want to speak directly to your reader in a conversational way or if you want to recount your story without involving your reader at all.

There are varying degrees to this.

This is how Issa Rae wrote her memoir, *The Misadventures of Awkward Black Girl.*

> My fellow awkward, once you step foot out of your own home, expect to be seen. It's inevitable. . . .
> The gamut of "blackness is so wide. So very, very wide. Luckily for you, I have encountered almost *every* type of black, and as the self-appointed representative of the "Awkward" Blacks, I am taking it

upon myself to not only introduce other Awkward Blacks to each type of black, but also to give them guidance on appropriately dealing with each type.

The humorous tone of her memoir makes this a good choice.

One Last Point

The mature self brings a measure of judgment into play. Note that there is a difference between judgment and being judgmental. Judgment is reason, the ability to analyze and make conclusions. Our mature self should show "good or insightful judgment" when pondering the past.

In our memoir, we need to share our insights, our judgments, about what happened. We are on a quest for knowledge, enlightenment, understanding, and readers want to hear what we've learned.

We might contrast how we viewed a situation years ago with how we view it now. Or we might note that when we did something, we had a wrong or bad attitude or perspective.

Mary Karr begins her memoir *Lit* with a prologue that is a letter to her son. Note her reflections:

> However long I've been granted sobriety, however many hours I logged in therapists' offices and the confessional, I've still managed to hurt you, and not just with the divorce when you were five, with its attendant shouting matches and slammed doors. . . .
> We both remember, albeit in varying tones of gray and black and brown, the misery I mired us in. . . . That's the story I want to tell: how I started getting drunk. How being drunk got increasingly hard, and being not drunk felt impossible.

No judging, just mature judgment—make that your aim.

Writing Prompt:

"No one in my family knows . . ."

_____

_____

_____

_____

_____

_____

_____

_____

_____

_____

_____

_____

_____

Chapter 10: Honest Recollection

Earlier in this workbook, we briefly touched on the need to present ourselves honestly. Part of that involves honest recollection: not exaggerating or twisting events to present ourselves in a favorable light or as evoke empathy as a victim.

We want readers to empathize, and if they sense we are lying or stretching the truth for dishonorable reasons, they will probably react negatively.

I use the word *dishonorable* because there are times we may want to stretch or embellish the truth for effect in a *harmless* way to make a story more entertaining. But the operative word is *intent*. We need to look at how and why we are presenting a memory and what our intention is in doing so.

We want to convey that we are sharing our story to the best of our recollection. Take a look at a passage from Domenica Ruta's memoir *With or Without You*. In this passage, she is six years old.

> I run back into the apartment and see my father on top of [my mother], his hands wrapped around her throat as he bangs her head against the thinly carpeted concrete floor. I jump on his back and pry him away, though that hardly seems possible now. Another fictive flight of memory? I don't know. But that is how I remember it, so that's what I'm telling you here. . . .
>
> Sometime after that encounter, I resumed my weekend visits at Dad's. It was as if nothing had happened. What I remember most about my father from then on was his absence.

Reflecting back on a time of abuse, Ruta writes in her memoir:

> I've tried so many times to make sense of my experience. Obliteration was the one that worked best. Pretend it never happened at all. . . . I don't remember many of the details now. But that can happen to any memory, toxic or not. If you can remember anything, it's already wrong. The image or event has changed, just as you have—minutely,

chemically, through the passage of time between then and now. Something happens to you, and then it's gone.

Notice how Ruta honestly shares her memories. She admits she isn't sure of the facts. How can she accurately recall all the details of events at such a young age?

But with a mature self looking back, she does her best to gather the impressions of memory and piece them together as honestly as she can.

This ties in with voice and tone, which we discussed in the previous chapter. If you are working on describing a moment in your past, and you can't recall some of the details, instead of making things up to fill in the blanks, admit this is your best recollection. Share your thoughts and impressions of that time. Speculate on the pieces you can't recall, but make it clear you are speculating. If you like, add emotional commentary. Your honesty or lack thereof is what will shine through.

Don't invent parts of your life or come up with "a better ending" to your story because you think it will be entertaining. That's what fiction is for, not memoir.

Practice writing with honest recollection.

Write about a moment in your past that you partially remember but that was impacting. As you describe it, convey this as an honest recollection, stating what you do and don't recall (details, feelings, etc.) and what you assume or guess at:

_____

_____

_____

_____

_____

_____

_____

_____

_____

_____

_____

_____

_____

_____

_____

_____

_____

_____

Just because we are telling the truth, that doesn't mean we tell _everything_. While we want to uncover and reveal, there may be things we are not comfortable with talking about. We may feel inclined to leave these things out of our stories. And that's perfectly fine.

Make a list of everything you consider taboo—things you will not discuss, even if they play an important part in your story:

_____

_____

_____

_____

_____

_____

_____

_____

_____

_____

_____

_____

_____

_____

Pray over these things. Ask God to help you discern what fears you might need to overcome or just push aside to be able to tell your story effectively. Ask God to show you how you might present painful events or issues in a way that won't cause you more pain.

Consider sharing some of these difficult memories with a trusted friend, and ask that person how much and what kind of detail they would be comfortable reading, if you described these memories in writing. Sometimes bouncing material off of an empathetic listener can give us perspective and help decide what to include and what to omit.

> "In sobriety, memories return slowly and in the wrong order. Often there's no trigger, just a rumble in my stomach or a fluttering in the rib cage, like a small animal is trapped inside and wants to find its way out. Pieces of dialogue, images, entire scenes sometimes spill out unexpectedly, then slither into the grass. I try to catch them, to see what more they have to say, only to watch them slip between my fingers. Pinning down a memory is like gathering a handful of water and trying to hold on. In the end, it's an act you can only mime."
>
> — *With or Without You*, Domenica Ruta

Writing Prompt: "I could never write about . . ."

_____

_____

_____

_____

_____

_____

_____

_____

_____

_____

_____

_____

_____

Part 3: Utilizing Cinematic Technique

Chapter 11: Bringing Your Story to Life with Sensory Detail

Just because you are "baring the truth," that doesn't mean it will be interesting to read. You could have the most amazing personal story to tell, but if you don't tell it well—if you don't transport your readers into your life—you may bore them to tears.

One good way to avoid this is by applying the fiction writers' adage: *Show, don't tell*. The more you can play out your "scenes" in a cinematic way, the more you'll immerse your reader in your story.

Try to imagine the events of your life playing out on a movie screen. Stop and picture the entire "stage" and note what details present themselves.

For example, instead of saying "Whenever my father came home every night, he terrorized our family," you might write:

> One night I sat at the table doing my math homework, when I heard the door swing open and my father's loud, drunk laugh. My blood went suddenly cold, and the pencil froze in my hand. I hadn't seen my father in months, and the last time he strode into the house, my mother landed in the hospital with a broken jaw. I prayed, thanking God that Mom was watching Jamal at his basketball game, but one look on my father's face as he came inside and spotted me made me cringe with fear. He would look for someone to take out his hurt and pain, and that someone would be me.

Writing with a cinematic style may be new and challenging to you, and it takes practice. If you picture the events of your life as movie scenes, it will help you bring the moment to life. Use dialogue and actions and show thoughts, playing out the "scene" in real time. Your story will be much more effective than if you just tell what happens.

Think about *specific* sensory details. Don't just say "she was beautiful." Consider *in what ways she was beautiful*. Think about what Toni Morrison says is "emotional memory—what the nerves and the skin remember as well as how it appeared."

Think of one of the important moments that you plan to have in your memoir. Write a brief paragraph summarizing what happened:

_____

_____

_____

_____

_____

_____

_____

_____

_____

_____

_____

Now, take a few minutes to close your eyes and play out the event in your head. The, describe it with sensory detail from a key starting point and "film" the first few moments, including your senses (sights, sounds, textures, smells, tastes), your thoughts, your emotions, your reactions.

_____

_____

_____

_____

_____

_____

_____

_____

_____

_____

_____

_____

_____

Strong Nouns and Verbs

To immerse readers in our stories, we want to avoid abstractions and generalizations. Use specifics. Use strong nouns and verbs instead of weak construction.

Instead of saying "the day was hot, and I was tired," try "the sweltering sun beat down on my shoulders, and I could hardly lift my feet to climb the twenty steps up to my apartment."

Here are some rich descriptions from memoirs:

> My first-grade teacher was Sister Agnes, a short, stern woman who had given up a large family fortune to become a nun. She wore pastel blouses and nylon shirts and beige sneakers whose soles had worn down over the years to a smooth, eerily silent rubber pad that allowed her to sneak up on her students unawares. . . . I could track the brown elastic of Sister Agnes's knee-highs as they slowly descended her thick veiny calves. (*With or Without You*, Domenica Ruta)

> Our house was chocolate-brown brick. There was an anemic tree in the front yard, and a tall deciduous tree in the back that fluttered purple and gray in the light of the city night sky. . . . The houses were so close together we found shade on hot days by sitting in the grassy spots between them. (*Men We Reaped*, Jesmyn Ward)

> After we took a number, we waited. And waited. . . . As we waited, the room filled up with dozens and dozens of Invisibles. Broken teeth, deep wrinkles, greasy hair, ill-fitting clothes. They all seemed to

belong together, and to understand each other. I was the one who was out of place here. I wondered if they felt as uncomfortable in my world as I felt in theirs. (*The Invisible Girls*, Sarah Thebarge)

He had to push aside the shiny loose papers torn from waiting-room magazines, old newspapers, empty cups, and long-ago-used bottles of motor oil and funnels that lived in the backseat to make room for me. He sang the seat belt song as he buckled me in, as was my rule. (*Coming Clean*, Kimberly Rae Miller)

Try using two or three senses in your descriptions. Here are some examples that use sensory detail effectively:

Smells:

> Even with the window open, the truck was redolent with Camel smoke and the goop Daddy used to clean oil off his hands with. There was a hint of cumin from a paper bag of corn-husk tamales from a roadside stand. And running under it all like current—what got him up in the morning and laid him out at night was the oak smell of wood barrels where whiskey soaked up the flavor.
>   . . . He drew a pint bottle from under his seat. He put the upended lid in the ashtray, and before he handed the bottle over, he drew out a corner of his shirttail to wipe the top with, saying, Want a swig? (*Lit*, Mary Karr)

Sounds:

> I put my head on Maya's chest, resting my cheek against the soft cotton of her gown. The rise and fall of her mechanically powered breath is like a whoosh of ocean tide—in and out, in and out. The steady drumming of her heart fills my senses. At last, I raise my head. There will be no last breath to signal the end. (*Swimming with Maya*, Eleanor Vincent)

Sensory detail can include the weather and the feeling of the air in a room, the lighting of a space, the feel of clothing on our bodies and the texture of sand and rocks under our feet, the taste of a cold thick milkshake going down a parched throat.

Sensory details bring a memory to life. Don't overdo it. Just a few strokes to trigger the senses is all that's needed.

Give this a try! Rewrite the following sentences (and embellish them with specifics) to bring in more visual and sensory details. Use your imagination.

"I was outside at night and I couldn't see anything."

_____

_____

_____

_____

_____

_____

_____

_____

_____

"My mother stood at the sink, washing dishes. She was mad."

_____

_____

_____

_____

_____

_____

_____

_____

_____

"I walked into the crowded doctor's office. There were lots of people sitting around."

_____

_____

_____

_____

_____

_____

_____

_____

_____

_____

"The teacher walked into the room. She looked mean."

_____

_____

_____

_____

_____

_____

_____

_____

_____

Try to avoid boring descriptions of people and places. The key to terrific description is to make it fresh and thoughtful, and reflect back on the person describing.

In other words, people and places and things in your chapters should be described through your eyes, through the lens of how you saw them and felt about them. Instead of giving a laundry list of eye color, height and build, and hair color, think of specific unique features and quirks and behaviors that you associate with each person.

Capturing the Era

Capturing the era or time periods in our memoir is another important detail we must not omit.

As you bring each incident to life, think about the date it took place. Not only do you need to bring the people and places to life, you need to accurately and tactilely reflect the time period.

What kinds of things were prominent back then: brands and styles of cars, tech (or lack thereof), products, songs, fads, stores, slogans (remember "Winston tastes good, like a cigarette should"?), commercials, magazines . . . ?

Dig deep into your memory and pull out those little pieces of the past that can help you re-create the era.

I can recall riding my Schwinn three-speed with a basket full of returnable Coke bottles to the main drag, where I would give them to the liquor store owner, and with the change buy five-cent Hershey bars and Sugar Daddy pops.

Maya Angelou describes the cotton-pickers coming into the general store her grandmother owned and ran in *I Know Why the Caged Bird Sings*:

> The sound of the empty cotton sacks dragging over the floor and the murmurs of waking people were sliced by the cash register as we rang up the five-cent sales.

Are you old enough to remember how hard it was to press down on typewriter keys? Or what it felt like to stick your finger in the holes of a rotary phone and dial a number?

Think about local, national, or world events that create the backdrop of your story. Pick one event and describe where you were on that day. Think of all the details that come to mind that represent that era. Write a passage describing that moment in a way that uses sensory detail to evoke the era:

_____

_____

_____

_____

_____

_____

_____

_____

_____

_____

_____

_____

_____

_____

Make a list of key historical events that you might include in your memoir:

_____

_____

_____

_____

_____

_____

_____

_____

_____

_____

_____

_____

Make a list of fads, popular songs, brand-name products, or other items from your past that you might include. Describe what they looked, felt, tasted, smelled like:

_____

_____

_____

_____

_____

_____

_____

_____

_____

_____

_____

_____

_____

_____

_____

How to Get Inspired to Write

- *Keep a journal.* Set a time *every day* to write a little in your journal. It can be the place to vent, to dig up memories, to ponder on your life lessons, and to get in the habit of writing.

- *Use writing prompts to get the creative juices flowing.* You can find countless writing prompts online (and some at the end of this book).

- *Connect with a local or online writing community.* The internet is full of places to connect with writers. Consider local writers' clubs or MeetUp groups so you can get to know other writers in your area.

- *Consider finding an accountability partner.* This doesn't have to be a writer, but it's encouraging to team up with another writer. You can motivate each other, set deadlines, and critique each other's work.

- *Play inspiring music, look at uplifting images.* When we expose ourselves to the beauty of creation, it can put us in the right mood to write.

- *Read excellent books: memoirs, novels, poetry, nonfiction.* Read widely. Glean from great authors how to write beautiful descriptions, catchy dialogue, powerful characters. Reading is a must!

- *Watch movies or documentaries of the eras and/or places you are writing about.* It helps to recall those details of the past if we see visuals to remind us. Reading books about those times and locales is *also helpful.*

- *Make a photo billboard or create some Pinterest boards.* These are some other ways to surround yourself with imagery. Images spark creativity. Practice describing some of the images in your journal. Experiment with words and phrasing.

Chapter 12: Character Arc

As with fiction, you want to show a strong character arc. Meaning, your starting point should show you with a specific outlook, mind-set, belief system, and/or attitude. The events that then transpire change you in profound ways so you gradually change. By the end of your story, your change should be front and center.

In fiction, we move our characters from their persona (the face they put on to deal with life and the world, which isn't authentic) to their true essence. Your story may showcase a similar arc.

Your Role as a Character

You are always the "main character" of your story, so you would be speaking in first-person point of view (POV), using "I" instead of "she."

In order to avoid having our memoir sound as if it's "all about me" and "look at what I've been through and how I've suffered," the character of "I" that you create for your memoir should be all about excavating memory in order to lead to self-awareness. And this learning curve or growth is portrayed in your character arc.

Memoir is about self-discovery, and if you don't show growth, change, and/or new self-awareness, your reader may feel cheated. The growth and insights you share are the rewards the reader gets for going with you on your journey.

Remember: the "I" of your story isn't the "you" of this moment. You are speaking from the mature self, reflecting back on the events in the past. You are, in a sense, creating a replica or clone of yourself through a filter.

The various experiences you share in your memoir will document this journey of change. Try to think of how, in every "scene" you include, you gained some insight, awareness, or lesson that contributed toward your change.

Describe the kind of person you were at the start of your story. Describe your attitudes about life, yourself, your family, or any pertinent topic:

_____

_____

_____

_____

_____

_____

_____

_____

_____

_____

Now describe how you were different at the end of your story or experience. What ways had you changed emotionally, physically, mentally, spiritually? Name the three most obvious changes:

_____

_____

_____

_____

_____

_____

_____

_____

What did you believe about yourself at the start of your story that changed by the end?

_____

_____

_____

_____

_____

_____

_____

_____

What we you able to do at the ending point of your story that you never would have been able to do at the start?

_____

_____

_____

_____

_____

_____

_____

_____

_____

_____

Tied in with the character arc is the focus on growth. In a novel, when a protagonist comes into her "essence" by the end of the story, it's because she's learned some lessons, gained insights into her problem and herself (and possibly others), and reflects on these changes.

Processing what has happens to us is not only a natural behavior, it's essential to show in our memoir so our readers can understand and witness the things we've come to understand about ourselves. And it's not just done at the end of our story but throughout.

Sarah Thebarger (*The Invisible* Girls) reflects on her Christian upbringing and how the stress of being a pastor's daughter coupled with expectations of perfection made her anxious and gave her panic attacks that sent her parents racing her to the hospital. A Christian counselor told her parents it was nothing that prayer and a few Bible verses couldn't fix.

Here's how she processes this at the end of her chapter:

> Even though I was just a teenager, it seemed unfair to me that fundamentalism could create severe angst that manifested as OCCD and panic disorder, and then proceed to decry the tolls created to assuage these tormenting conditions. . . .
> At times that feels like an overly critical assessment of an earnest but misguided community, until I remember that I was so afraid of God and all other authority figures that I had panic attacks and wet the bed a few times a week until I left for college.

Go back and read the passage you wrote at the start of the prior chapter (p. 79), when you chose one event and put in sensory detail.

Think awhile about that event, then write a paragraph or two of processing: stepping back and considering what you learned and experienced and how that impacted you.

_____

_____

_____

_____

_____

_____

_____

_____

_____

Your Cast of Characters

Just as we change in life, the people in our lives change. Not all do. But as you consider the important people in your story, think about how what you went through may have changed others. Then find places to show those changes in your story.

Your memoir, unless it's about an experience you went through utterly alone (such as surviving a year shipwrecked on an island void of people), should have other "characters."

We need to avoid the tendency to make our memoir "all about me." We shouldn't leave out or minimize the role others play in our story.

But just as with all other aspects of your memoir, you need to be selective. You don't want to bore readers with a list of dozens of relatives and their descriptions and ages. As in a great movie or novel, there are key "players" that act as ally, romantic interest, antagonist, or nemesis.

Some characters are secondary, there as backdrop, perhaps mentioned in order to provide a rich context for a situation you want to share. Focus on the people who impacted you, for good or ill, in a given situation.

Make a list of the key people in your memoir and, in one sentence, describe the overall role each plays (support, antagonist, etc.)

_____

_____

_____

_____

_____

_____

_____

_____

_____

**Choose four of those people and describe each one starting with the
sentence "[Name] was the kind of person who would . . ."**

_____

_____

_____

_____

_____

_____

_____

_____

_____

_____

_____

_____

_____

_____

_____

_____

_____

Take a few moments and describe the key person in your story, the one who impacted you the most, and elaborate in what way they impacted you as relates to the theme of your memoir:

_____

_____

_____

_____

_____

_____

_____

_____

Did they change over the course of your memoir's timeline? If so, in what way? If not, was that a "good" thing or a "bad" thing? Explain:

_____

_____

_____

_____

_____

_____

_____

_____

Writing Prompt:

"My memoir describes what I went through in order to . . ."

_____

_____

_____

_____

_____

_____

_____

_____

_____

_____

_____

_____

_____

_____

_____

_____

Chapter 13: Writing Authentic Dialogue

Dialogue is the epitome of "showing" instead of telling. Dialogue brings characters to life and engages readers. If we have no dialogue in our "scenes," those long descriptive paragraphs will get boring.

Dialogue adds "white space" to our pages, makes the reading move quickly, and helps keep our story from becoming cumbersome.

But dialogue can be boring, right? And who can accurately remember every word of a conversation? If you've ever had a fight with a friend or spouse, you know that it only takes a minute or two to forget something that had just been said—especially when it's a hot, emotional argument. I've often blurted, "But you just said . . . !" and my spouse replied, "No way! I did not!"

Needless to say, we often have selected memory.

Unless you have tape-recorded every moment of your past, you are not going to remember, word for word, what was said.

And here's another point: you wouldn't want to repeat exactly what was said in a given situation, because, for the most part, much of what we say is boring and repetitive.

Fiction writers learn the technique of *distilling* dialogue. What this means is exactly what it sounds like. Dialogue should present the gist of what needs to be said, minus the *ums* and *uhs* and unimportant stuff. No one likes to engage in boring conversation, so it stands to follow they wouldn't want to read it either.

Adding in realistic, dynamic, maybe humorous dialogue is the key to a terrific memoir.

Don't be afraid to "put words in someone's mouth," even your own. That's what you have to do. That's what good memoirists do. You want to be true and faithful to the *intent* of what's being said, and honestly represent those who are speaking.

Recall the conversations to the best of your ability. We all know we have memories that are like colanders—a lot slips out.

As you write dialogue, be sure each person sounds authentic, like himself or herself. Their speech should reflect their education, upbringing, and all the factors that make them who they are.

Here's a great exercise to get you thinking about dialogue: go to a public place, like a coffee shop or a mall and eavesdrop (respectfully). Listen to how people talk. It's funny that we don't tend to pay attention to the way people speak: their diction, vocabulary, sentence structure.

Study other memoirs to see what kind of dialogue they contain.

Here's a great example of effective, tight dialogue, from Kimberly Rae Miller's *Coming Clean*:

> "Wow, you girls did a great job," my mother said.
> I didn't say anything. I couldn't say anything. I was so angry with them for living this way again.
> Rachel took over, talking to my mother about her plans for grad school and her summer job working as a dockmaster on Fire Island.
> I watched my father look for some sign of his papers, under couch cushions or in coat pockets. Something to find comfort in.
> After Rachel left, the questions started coming.
> "Where did you put my box of old Day-Timers?"
> "I hope you didn't throw out my ice-cream maker; it only needed one part to work again."
> I didn't say anything.
> "Oh, you're not talking to us," my mom said as if I were seven years old again and being adorably rebellious.
> "I'm not talking," I said. "The refrigerator still needs cleaning."

Notice how tight and concise the dialogue is, interspersed with brief lines of narrative and action. The writer uses *said* because that verb, to readers, is "invisible." We *blip* over it so that it doesn't snag our attention, and that's important.

Use speech verbs like *said* and *asked*, instead of fancy verbs, such as extrapolated, cajoled, and elucidated. Those words will distract readers instead of allowing the dialogue to flow naturally.

You don't need to use a speech verb with every line, if it's clear who is speaking. Add in beats for reaction where reaction is needed. As we speak to people, we pause to process at certain times. We want our dialogue to reflect this natural behavior. If we don't, the dialogue will be rapid-fire, sounding more like a comedy sketch than real life.

Here's another good example of authentic, effective dialogue from Issa Rae's memoir. Notice how some of the pertinent information is quickly summarized so that only the key parts of the conversation are played out. Pay attention to those pauses she inserts for processing:

> "I don't think you like me very much," he started.
> "What? What are you talking about," I asked.
> "Oftentimes, I will call you and you won't call me back. Or when I come over to spend time with you, you'll just go to sleep . . . What are we doing?"
> As I listened to him go on about what he wasn't getting from me in our "relationship," I grew confused—what was this?
> I opted for the truth. "Honestly, I thought we were just . . ." What were the French words for "friends with benefits"?
> "What did you think we were 'just'?" he insisted.
> I scrambled to put words together without sounding vulgar. It was the first language-barrier issue we'd encountered. I kept repeating the words in English, hoping he'd understand . . . but the more and more I said it, the dumber I felt. Frustrated, he proposed a solution. "I think we should stop seeing each other, since you don't like me."
> I was shocked. I had never been broken up with before, much less from someone with whom I didn't even know I was in a relationship.
> . . .
> "If that's what you think is best."

Notice, also, that when writing dialogue, every time you switch speakers, you begin a new paragraph. That is the simplest way to be clear who is speaking.

Imagine a key conversation in your memoir. Try writing some of the dialogue. Be sure to note who is speaking and intersperse with bits of narrative and processing (reacting):

_____

_____

_____

_____

_____

_____

_____

_____

_____

_____

_____

_____

_____

_____

_____

_____

_____

_____

_____

_____

_____

Fiction-Writing Tips

- *Don't give away too much too soon.* Readers love suspense and mystery. Set up the problems, your hopes and dreams, and your fears early on, then play out your story. Your reader will now want to see if you reached those dreams or overcame those fears.

- *As you "play out" your scenes, be sure to show the natural cycle of action-reaction.* When something happens, we react. The first reaction is visceral, emotional. Then we move into processing what just happened. Processing prompts a new decision, which leads to a new action. If it helps, write this on a card you tape next to your computer screen: action-reaction-process-decision-new action.

- *Show the emotion instead of naming it.* Think about how you felt and describe the feelings and thoughts you had in any given moment. It's always better to say something like "Heat flushed my face and I wanted to crawl under a rock when he called me to the front of the room" instead of "When he called me to the front of the room, I was embarrassed and self-conscious."

- *Intersperse dialogue, narrative, and action.* Avoid going on for pages with any of these elements; instead, alternate to keep the reading interesting.

- *Avoid overwriting.* Be willing to cut lines, paragraphs, even whole scenes. A writer needs to look at each section and ask: "Do I need this?" Overly wordy sentences, extended paragraphs, and repetition should all be removed.

- *Try to eliminate hedging words.* Hedging words, such as seemed, sort of, perhaps, slightly, somewhat—weaken writing. Rather than saying "She noticed that he seemed to be angry," try "She startled at his harsh words.

Writing Prompt:

"All my life, I believed that _____ , but it took _____ to happen for me to learn the truth . . ."

_____

_____

_____

_____

_____

_____

_____

_____

_____

_____

_____

_____

_____

Conclusion

Hopefully, by the time you've gotten to the end of this workbook, you've made good progress on your memoir. You've organized your content. You've perhaps come up with a working title. You've chosen a structure.

Maybe you've already written some chapters! Every small step is a huge accomplishment. Be proud of those achievements.

If you've been finding the process painful, either because of the writing challenges or the memories that are being dredged up (or both), don't give up! If God has moved you to write your story, know that He is with you every step of the way.

Keep praying. Ask for clarity, for courage, for peace. Stick with it. Determine a writing schedule and be faithful to it. Get an accountability partner, if that will help you make steady progress on your memoir.

Your memoir isn't going to write itself, nor will God write it for you. If you're lacking in skills, seek out resources (classes, podcasts, books, workshops) to help you gain the needed skills or assistance.

It can be of great help and encouragement to hire an editor or writing coach to work with you along the way. Consider having someone professional take a look at your chapter outline before you get into the writing. Or write a couple of chapters and have them critiqued. Getting feedback, especially early on, will shine a light on your weak elements, and with expert guidance you'll learn to master the craft of writing strong chapters with sensory detail, dialogue, narrative, and thoughtful introspection.

More than anything, find joy in the writing journey. The creative expression of storytelling shouldn't be a miserable experience. If it is, maybe now is not your season to write.

When you think your book is finished, you'll be ready to look into publishing options, and there are plenty of people and countless books and blog posts to help you take those next steps.

But don't get distracted by jumping the gun and worrying about publishing and marketing before you've finished your book. Focus on writing the best story you can, because everything we do, we should do for God's glory. And that means taking care to be diligent, patient, and open to His leading for each step along the way.

My prayer is that you will now be inspired, excited, and determined to write your story, from start to finish, and that through this process you will not only experience deep self-discovery but will also see God's hand directing you on your path.

> Before a word is on my tongue, you, Lord, know it completely. You hem me in behind and before, and you lay your hand upon me. Such knowledge is too wonderful for me, too lofty for me to attain. (Psalm 139:4–6 NIV)

"When you tell your story, an extraordinary universe is revealed. As a mature person encountering a younger self, you change. Past experiences, even poignant ones, enrich the present, because you are not simply observing and reporting—you are participating in reliving. If you've ever had any doubts about your life's true purpose, writing your story will help you discover it."

— *Your Life Is a Book*, Brenda Peterson & Sarah Jane Freymann

Additional Writing Prompts

To help you get your writing juices flowing, take a few minutes when you sit down to work on your memoir to freewrite. Using prompts like these help spark memories and emotions. Some of what you write might be just what you need to put in your memoir!

If you want to write longer entries, grab a journal or open up a Word document on your computer and let the writing flow!

"I had never been more afraid than on the day when . . ."

_____

_____

_____

_____

_____

"I had never been more proud than on the day when . . ."

_____

_____

_____

_____

_____

_____

"I had never been more sorry than on the day when . . ."

_____

_____

_____

_____

_____

_____

"I had never been more joyous than on the day when . . ."

_____

_____

_____

_____

_____

"If I had been more careful or thought first, I wouldn't have . . ."

_____

_____

_____

_____

_____

"I had never been more afraid than on the day when . . ."

_____

_____

_____

_____

"In my family, it was assumed . . ."

_____

_____

_____

_____

_____

_____

"I tried hard to keep secret . . ."

_____

_____

_____

_____

_____

_____

"I was shocked when I learned . . ."

_____

_____

_____

_____

_____

_____

"I was so naïve; I had no idea that . . ."

_____

_____

_____

_____

_____

_____

"I felt the most safe when . . ."

_____

_____

_____

_____

_____

_____

_____

"Nothing frightened me more than . . ."

_____

_____

_____

_____

_____

_____

_____

Recommended Reading

Memoirs (alphabetical order)

A Long Way Gone: Memoirs of a Boy Soldier by Ishmael Beah

A Moveable Feast by Ernest Hemingway

All Over But the Shoutin' by Rick Bragg

An Interrupted Life: The Diaries of Etty Hillesum by Etty Hillesum

Angela's Ashes by Frank McCourt

Astonished by Beverly Donofrio

Autobiography of a Face by Lucy Grealy

Born Standing Up by Steve Martin

Colored People by Henry Louis Gates Jr.

Coming About, A Family Passage at Sea by Susan Tyler Hitchcock

Coming Clean by Kimberly Rae Miller

Cultivate by Lara Casey

Eat, Pray, Love by Elizabeth Gilbert

Girl Meets God by Lauren F. Winner

Hillbilly Elegy: A Memoir of a Family and Culture in Crisis by J. D. Vance

I Know Why the Caged Bird Sings by Maya Angelou

In Country by Bobbie Ann Mason

Jesus Land by Julia Sheeres

Mama Makes Up Her Mind: And Other Dangers of Southern Living by Bailey White

Manic: A Memoir by Terri Cheney

Men We Reaped by Jesmyn Ward

Molina by Benjie Molina and Joan Ryan

My Life in France by Julia Child

Out of Africa by Karen Blixen

Pack of Two: The Intricate Bond between People and Dogs by Carolyn Knapp

Pilgrim at Tinker Creek by Annie Dillard

Reason for Hope: A Spiritual Journey by Jane Goodall

Running with Scissors by Augusten Burroughs

Still Woman Enough: A Memoir by Loretta Lynn

Swimming with Maya: A Mother's Story by Eleanor Vincent

The Dance of the Dissident Daughter by Sue Monk Kidd

The Glass Castle by Jeannette Walls

The Invisible Girls by Sarah Thebarge

The Misadventures of Awkward Black Girl by Issa Rae

The Year of Magical Thinking by Joan Didion

This Boy's Life by Tobias Wolff

Traveling Mercies by Anne Lamott

Two or Three Things I Know for Sure by Dorothy Allison

Wit: A Memoir by Mary Karr

On Writing Memoirs

If You Want to Write by Brenda Ueland

Inventing the Truth: The Art and Craft of Memoir by William Zinsser (editor)

The Art of Memoir by Mary Karr

The Power of Memoir: How to Write Your Healing Story by Linda Myers

Your Life Is a Book: How to Craft & Publish Your Memoir by Peterson and Freymann

Your Story: How to Write It So Others Will Want to Read It by Joanne Fedler

Writing Life Stories by Bill Roorbach

Chapter Outline: *The Invisible Girls*

Double Parallel Timeline Example

It can be very helpful to summarize and outline a memoir that is using a structure that might work for your story.

Sarah Thebarge's memoir, *The Invisible Girls*, uses two timelines, and she organized the material in a logical manner that showcases her themes and helps use her story as a lens to telling her present account of meeting and coming to love a Somali woman and her five young daughters.

Both timelines move forward in chronological order.

Another way memoir can be laid out is by using a roll of butcher paper. Roll out a long section of the white paper, then draw a horizontal line bisecting the section. That's your timeline. If you have two timelines, create two parallel lines. You can write each scene or memory on a sticky note, then place it on the appropriate timeline (that way you can move them around).

Doing this helps you see the bigger picture of your memoir. When all the pieces are in the right places, you can create an outline like this, or use numbered index cards (my favorite) for each chapter. Write one scene or chapter per index card, they lay them out in order on a table. This gives you a "big picture" of your whole story, and you can move them around as needed before you begin writing.

If Sarah had told her story in just one timeline, detailing her childhood, her engagement, her horrific trauma of her cancer, and her recovery, *and then* telling how she met this family, it wouldn't have worked nearly as well. Since both timelines cover a specific capsule of time, each ending with deep insights, lessons learned, and epiphanies, this structure is perfect.

Take a look at this summary of her memoir. This should give you a roadmap to laying out your memoir, as well as helping you see how you might summarize other memoirs to help you determine the structure that would best suit your story.

1. **Timeline 1. One year ago.** [This sets the early timeline]. Sarah meets the Somali family on the train in Portland and, moved by compassion for their condition, asks for their address.

2. **Two years earlier.** She describes how, after eighteen months of grueling breast cancer surgeries, she moved from CT to OR. A quick overview of her treatments, near death, and utter despondency led her to this decision to move, and she arrives in Portland, facing uncertainty, feeling invisible.

3. **Soon after arriving in Portland.** Her doctor tells her she'll probably be infertile and should get a hysterectomy. She is with her friend Katrina, who has two small children, thinking of how she will never have children of her own and is losing every part that defines her as a woman.

4. **Timeline 1.** Sarah gets up the nerve to visit the Somali family, bringing cookies. She is stunned to see an empty apartment. The five girls are endearing. The family has nothing.

5. **Timeline 1.** In response, Sarah researched info on Somalia and aid. She visits again, bringing supplies and more food. They are starving.

6. **Timeline 2. [This is where she begins the backstory in order].** Early memories of her childhood, establishing her family, her father as a pastor.

7. **Timeline 2.** Reflections of growing up in church, how women were kept subservient.

8. **Timeline 2.** How she and her brothers pretended to be good children but were mischievous and gossipy about the church members.

9. **Timeline 1.** Sarah visits the family, takes some of the girls to the market, stunned at their behavior and lack of understanding basic living in America.

10. **Timeline 2.** How her parents raised her with tough love, but also with so much pressure she had panic attacks and a fear of failing.

11. **Timeline 1.** She makes pasta for the family and starts growing close to them.

12. **Timeline 2.** Reflects on her teen years, when she had ambitions for her life, but those around her expected her to aim for a traditional wife and mother role.

13. **Timeline 2.** Talks about her sister Hannah, who had multiple heart surgeries. Sarah decides to go to college in Los Angeles to study medicine. She realizes how sheltered she's been and meets Katrina, who becomes a close friend. She begins feeling free.

14. **Timeline 1.** Sarah is over at the family's apartment, sharing food and playing, when one of the girls defecates on the floor (and the family ignores it). Horrified, Sarah leaves.

15. **Timeline 2.** Works hard in college, more aware of gender discrepancies and church failings.

16. **Timeline 2.** Has a crisis in college, realizing she wants to write, not become a doctor. Applies to Yale for pre-med to be a physician's assistant.

17. **Timeline 2.** She gets accepted and eventually graduates, the first woman in her family to get a master's degree.

18. **Timeline 2.** She starts working, takes journalism classes at Columbia, meets Ian at a Bible study. He's wonderful, rich, successful, and they plan to marry in a year, when she graduates from Columbia. The pinnacle of happiness before it all comes crashing down.

19. **Timeline 1.** Sarah struggles with doubts about helping the Somali family, then reads an article about young Somali girls being accused as spies and murdered. She decides to commit, work past her discomfort, and help the family. She learns the mother, Hadhi, in her twenties, had also had three sons, who died. Compassion grows.

20. **Timeline 2.** During her last year of journalism studies, she notices blood leaking from her nipple. It's cancer. She can't believe it—she's only twenty-seven. She cries and prays.

21. **Timeline 2.** Ian is supportive. Her parents visit. No one can help.

22. **Timeline 2.** Church members are supportive: pray, sing, and try to encourage her.

23. **Timeline 2.** She has two weeks before her double mastectomy. She cries in Ian's arms.

24. **Timeline 2.** Angry at God, Ian and her parents watch as she goes into surgery.
25. **Timeline 1.** Sarah learns the government aid is being cut off. She asks about the father, who abandoned them.
26. **Timeline 1.** Sarah questions Hadhi about her husband, learned he was violent and they are hiding from him.
27. **Timeline 2.** Wakes from surgery. In terrible pain.
28. **Timeline 2.** Drugs, more pain, trying to wake from surgery,
29. **Timeline 2.** Leaves hospital, gets her meds.
30. **Timeline 1.** Sarah realizes the family doesn't know how to turn on heat, has no towels. She tells them she is going on a trip for a week and they panic.
31. **Timeline 2.** Recovering. Parents helping Sarah. Angry at God, wondering what she ate or did that gave her cancer.
32. **Timeline 2.** A few months after surgery, trying to adjust. A professor friend named Libby also has cancer. They console each other. They are both angry at God. She tries to believe He loves her.
33. **Timeline 2.** Sarah tries to go back to school. Libby has many surgeries. She's upset that Ian is backing away and "can't deal with this."
34. **Timeline 1.** Sarah helps Hadhi, who is out of money and can't pay bills or buy food. They drive to the DHS office.
35. **Timeline 2.** Libby is getting worse. Ian takes Sarah to a holiday party. He tries to cheer her up, but it doesn't help.
36. **Timeline 2.** Sarah flies home for Christmas. Ian throws her a birthday party. She is not okay. She blows out the candles and catches her hair on fire.
37. **Timeline 1.** At the DHS office they can't get any help. Sarah tells Hadhi they'll figure something out.
38. **Timeline 2.** Ian and Sarah go to Mexico a few months later, before she undergoes reconstructive surgery. She is angry at her body and God for betraying her.
39. **Timeline 2.** Sarah feels her faith is gone. Ian is with her and they talk about the long year. She believes it is almost over after this last surgery, trying to be hopeful.

40. **Timeline 1.** Sarah celebrates Somali Christmas with the family.

41. **Timeline 2.** After Mexico, Sarah has surgery. Then is told her cancer is back. More surgery, chemo, radiation. She pleads with God to die. Learns Libby died.

42. **Timeline 1.** Sarah, at the Somali apartment, has to explain why you can't call 911 for fun or order pizza without paying for it. They have so much to learn about living in America.

43. **Timeline 1.** Sarah realizes the girls are treated badly at school. Chaki is sick and she comes over to help. She is getting more attached to this family.

44. **Timeline 2.** Before chemo, Sarah cuts her hair off. Ian doesn't like it. He breaks up with her, saying he "can't handle it." As if she could. The hurt and anger rage.

45. **Timeline 1.** Sarah takes the Somali family to a Thanksgiving dinner.

46. **Timeline 1.** Sarah enlists her church to collect money for the family. Sadaka is missing her father.

47. **Timeline 2.** Sarah goes through the grueling rounds of chemo, feeling she has lost everything and everyone. Then more cancer is found.

48. **Timeline 2.** Six weeks of radiation and feeling horribly depressed.

49. **Timeline 2.** Sarah ponders the "why" and worries that if she begs God to tell her the answer, he would say, "because I said so," and she would hate him.

50. **Timeline 1.** The Somali family is struggling. They can't pay bills; everything breaks. Hadhi dresses Sarah up in Somali clothing. Sarah assures them she will help them get through. (Note the parallel of Sarah's deepest despair in the past timeline and Hadhi's matching despair in the more present timeline.)

51. **Timeline 1.** When Sarah sees the milk is spoiled in the family's fridge, she realizes they don't understand how it works. They've kept the door open for weeks.

52. **Timeline 1.** Sarah eats Somali food with the family. Hahdi doesn't know when the girls were born. The bills aren't paid. Sarah is overwhelmed.

53. **Timeline 2.** She reflects back to growing up and views of women and sex. How someone at her college asked her to donate her eggs, saying she'd be paid a lot for them.

54. **Timeline 1.** Sarah watches TV with the family, seeing their reactions. Hadhi sees a violent man and says that is how her husband is.

55. **Timeline 1.** Sarah teaches basics to the family: how to take care of washing, food, hygiene, to arithmetic to shop, money, etc.

56. **Timeline 1.** Hadhi is sick, so Sarah takes her to an Emergency room. Hadhi says it's her malaria. She is falling apart.

57. **Timeline 1.** At the hospital, Hadhi gets help. A woman who is a Somali interpreter helps her, giving her and Sarah hope for a bright future for refugees like them in America.

58. **Timeline 1.** They get Hadhi's meds and food. Sarah realizes she hasn't really looked at Hadhi and how hard she's had it. She is an invisible girl too.

59. **Timeline 2.** After chemo and radiation, she has pneumonia that is getting worse. Ian is out of the picture. She is dying. Her friend Rajah reads her Psalm 23.

60. **Timeline 2.** She's in the hospital for two weeks, her family comes. Since she is dying, she wants to check out and go to her brother's wedding.

61. **Timeline 2.** Her pneumonia worsens. She prays and prays for God to help her.

62. **Timeline 2.** Sarah and Ian meet and she discovers he's been having sex with another woman. He feels ashamed, and she says, "Wasn't I worth anything to you?"

63. **Timeline 2.** Ian takes her to the airport. She is off to Portland, on new meds, determined to start a new life. Hoping to find God again.

64. **Timeline 2.** She arrives in Portland, works at the ER, gets an apartment, attends a church. Weeks go by but she feels hopeless.

65. **Timeline 1.** Sarah takes a couple of the girls for an outing. They go to Starbucks and a park, and Sarah realizes how little they understand life in America.

66. **Timeline 1.** Hadhi is still sick. She and a friend take the girls to Chuck E. Cheese. She sees how mothers glare at her with these Somali girls.

67. **Timeline 2.** She gets a call from her OB/GYN saying she should have a hysterectomy. She recalls a social worker explaining that we are like ants to God and sometimes he can't help but step on a few.

68. **Timeline 1.** Sarah takes some of the girls out again, and they act up and don't understand how to behave. Sarah realizes she needs to teach them a lot and decides to enlist other women to help.

69. **Timeline 1.** Sarah now has help. The women take the girls to the park.

70. **Timeline 1.** Sarah hears a man has been visiting the family and they are moving to Seattle. Then Sarah can't reach Hadhi, and they are not home. She has no way to find them.

71. **Timeline 1.** A week later, finally someone is in the apartment. Hadhi and her husband come in. The girls make Sarah sit in the closet. The man finds her.

72. **Timeline 1.** Sarah learns they are moving to Seattle and they talk about having a party to say good-bye. She reflects on all the love she's gotten from this family and how it's saved her. She hates to lose them.

73. **Timeline 1.** Sarah goes with food to wish them good-by. One of the girls cries, and Sarah promises she will always love her and will find her wherever she goes.

74. **Timeline 1.** Sarah gives them a card with her contact info. The other women come for the party. She says good-bye and cries while driving home.

75. **Timeline 1.** Time goes on, she misses them and talks with them on the phone. She promises to visit soon.

76. **Timeline 2.** Six months after arriving in Portland, she watches a doctor sit by quietly while her own daughter gets an IV. It makes her think of God being close but not doing anything. When it's over, the doctor/mom then comforts the child. Is God like this too? She finally realizes God has been with her all along.

77. **Timeline 2.** Sarah goes back to CT thinking she will go home and to school there, since her year is up. But it doesn't feel right and show

121

goes back to Portland. She prays for God's direction and feels surrendered. It's in God's hands.

78. **Timeline 1.** Somehow all Sarah's contacts are erased from her phone. She has no way of getting in touch with the Somali family. Finally one of the girls calls but can't tell Sarah exactly where they are living. She has the girl give the phone to a neighbor, who tells Sarah the name of the apartment complex.

79. **Timeline 1.** Sarah heads to Seattle and after going to the wrong place, finds the right apartment. A happy reunion.

80. **Timeline 1.** After a happy visit, Sarah decides the way to help the girls is to raise money for them to go to college.

81. **Timeline 2.** Deciding to make Portland her home, she buys a house, but walking in with the keys, she feels so lonely and her dreams have been destroyed. The house is empty and she feels she should go find homeless people and invite them to live with her.

82. **Timeline 1.** Sarah takes a trip to Paris. Upon coming home, she knows God has healed her and given her a second chance at life. *As she rides on the train home, she meets the Somali family* (bringing the story full circle, to where she started the book).

83. **Epilogue.** Sarah meets a woman at night, a streetwalker. She helps her out, tells her about God, realizes invisible girls are everywhere.

I hope you see here how this double timeline works so effectively. Sarah has two stories to tell that are linked thematically with the idea of invisible girls. Her timeline shares how she felt invisible to her community, her boyfriend, her family, her church, and God. It shows the journey she went from hope to despair to faith.

The timeline with the family shows Sarah's journey to not only help them but reveal how, in helping them, she helped herself. Through them she learned about herself and God.

The two timelines meet up at the end, with Sarah's past timeline arriving at the moment she meets the family on the train, which is where the first timeline started.

About the Author

C. S. Lakin is a multipublished award-winning novelist and writing coach who loves to help writers find joy and success in their novel-writing journey. She works full-time as a copyeditor (fiction and nonfiction) and critiques about two hundred manuscripts a year. She teaches writing workshops around the country and gives instruction on her award-winning blog **Live Write Thrive** (www.livewritethrive.com). For manuscript critiques, visit Lakin's critique website **Critique My Manuscript** (critiquemymanuscript.com).

Lakin lives in a small town south of San Francisco, CA, with her husband Lee, a gigantic lab named Coaltrane, and three persnickety cats. She loves to hike and backpack, cook, watch basketball, and spend time with her two daughters and grandson. But most of all, she loves her Creator and her savior, Jesus Christ, and loves to bring glory to the One who gives life, breath, creativity, and story to His children.

Did you find this book helpful? The best way to thank a writer is to leave a positive, honest review. Be sure to leave a review for this book online that will help other writers learn how to tell their story for God's glory!

Made in the USA
Columbia, SC
24 May 2022

60839542R00072